TARTUFFE

By MOLIÈRE

Translated by CURTIS H. PAGE

Introduction by JOHN E. MATZKE

Tartuffe
By Molière (Jean-Baptiste Poquelin)
Translated by Curtis Hidden Page
Introduction by John E. Matzke

Print ISBN 13: 978-1-4209-5531-6
eBook ISBN 13: 978-1-4209-5532-3

This edition copyright © 2017. Digireads.com Publishing.

Cover Image: a detail of "Ducroisy in the title role of Tartuffe in 1668", from 'Costumes de Theatre de 1600 a 1820' by L. Lecomte, engraved by Francois Seraphin Delpech (1778-1825) (colour litho), Hippolyte Lecomte (1781-1857) (after) / Bibliotheque de L'Arsenal, Paris, France / Bridgeman Images.

Please visit *www.digireads.com*

CONTENTS

ACT IV.

ACT V.

Introduction

THE ORIGIN AND SPIRIT OF THE PLAY

To appreciate Molière's *Tartuffe* it is necessary to understand the genesis of the play, its moral significance and the importance which was attached to it by the men and women who witnessed its first representations.

Tartuffe is a hypocrite who under the cover of religious zeal and the interests of heaven serves his own most selfish ends, tries to rob the wife of his benefactor of her honor and brings discord and ruin into the family that had received him. The question is whether hypocrisy and piety have been sufficiently distinguished, or whether true religion has not after all been indirectly held up to scorn.

It is possible to outline the causes which induced Molière to select hypocrisy as the subject of a play at this period of his career. The main business of comedy for him was to show men their failings so that they might learn to correct them, and after some farces and comedies of the Italian type he had found his true sphere in the *Précieuses Ridicules* of the year 1659, which was followed in rapid succession by *Sganarelle*, *L'École des Maris*, *Les Fâcheux*, and *L'École des Femmes*, and each new play added to the number of his enemies. It was the Précieuses and the Marquis who had thus far suffered particularly, and their anger was fanned by envious authors who instinctively recognized the superiority of the new star that had risen above the literary horizon. The *École des Femmes* more than any of the earlier plays aroused strong opposition, and Molière in his defense wrote the *Critique de l'École des Femmes* and the *Impromptu de Versailles*, in both of which he dealt the strongest blows to those that had attacked him.

Among the various criticisms brought against him was his attitude toward religion. A remark of Gorgibus in *Sganarelle*, scene 1, had aroused opposition. Here *la Guide des Pécheurs* of the Spanish Dominican Luis de Granada, a book of pious teaching much in vogue among the devout of the time, was cited in a way to cause laughter as a more suitable book for young women than Mlle de Scudéry's novel *Clélie*. Then came the *École des Femmes* with its sermon on the duties of marriage and its suggestion of the ten commandments in the ten *Maximes du Mariage* in Act III, scene 2. Here the offense was more flagrant and the attack upon Molière became more violent. He was loudly accused of insulting religion, in fact this charge found definite expression in De Visé's *Zélinde, ou la véritable Critique de l'École des Femmes*, Aug. 4, 1663 as well as in Boursault's *Portrait du Peintre ou la contre-critique de l'École des Femmes*, Nov. 17, 1663. But even before it here appeared in print, it had been loudly pressed and Molière had taken cognizance of it in the *Critique de l'École des Femmes*, scene 7. He answered that the so-called sermon was not that, but only a *discours moral*, that it was certain that the truly pious that had heard it had found no cause for criticism, and that whatever religious phraseology occurred in it was justified by the nature of the character that spoke it. He touched upon this whole question here only as it were in passing, but there can be no question of its connection with the composition of *Tartuffe* which was first played on May 12 of the following year. Having been aroused to see religious hypocrisy in this empty criticism, he resolved to make a hypocrite the center of his next play.

It must be granted also that the religious condition of the country offered abundant opportunity for the serious study of this human failing. Religious shamming was without question encouraged by the conditions at the court. The young king, frivolous and pleasure loving, was convinced that the authority of the church must be upheld, and submitted often with evident reluctance to its influence. His religious guides belonged to the society of the Jesuits, which was in control of the Sorbonne and altogether the most influential of the religious orders of the country. The queen mother Anne of Austria and her immediate circle used every means in their power to augment the influence of the Church, and the consequence was a certain outward show of religious zeal in which self-interest often weighed more heavily than honest conviction.

In addition, the Jesuits had become responsible for teachings calculated to encourage a semblance of piety at variance with the secret intentions of the heart. The dangerous elements in this attitude were particularly evident in the Spaniard Escobar's book entitled *Moralis Theologia*, which had appeared in Lyon in 1646 and passed rapidly through 36 editions. Here the famous Jesuit doctrines of the *direction d'intention* and of the *restrictions mentales* were followed out to their logical end. To kill is a crime. Yet to walk where one's enemy lies in waiting, and with the intention not of meeting him but of enjoying the landscape though armed for the emergency is quite innocent, and a duel if accepted becomes an act of legitimate self defense. To lie is a sin, but it can be neutralized by a proper mental restriction, as when a priest swears that he has not heard a certain matter in the confessional, adding in his heart that he has not heard it in his capacity as a private individual.

The reform movement, on the other hand, had its center in the Jansenists of the Port Royal. The keynote of their teaching was that of the Reformation in general, though they never broke their connection with the Catholic Church. They maintained that man can be redeemed from sin only by the direct intervention of the grace of God. The growth of their influence caused a bitter attack upon them by the

Jesuits, and the outcome of this battle fought with passion on either side was the publication in 1656 and 1657 of Pascal's famous *Lettres Provinciales*, in which the casuistic doctrines of the Jesuits were analyzed with keen logic and biting satire. In the seventh and ninth of these letters the questions of the purity of intention and mental reservation are analyzed in detail, and their publication did much to increase the animosity of the conflict.

The result of all these discussions was that the play, when it appeared, was accepted as taking sides. Yet it must be remembered that we know nothing directly of Molière's personal attitude to the questions involved. No conclusions should be drawn from his early training in the Jesuit Collège de Clermont or from the contrary influence of Gassendi's teaching upon him or from his evident knowledge of and indebtedness to the *Lettres Provinciales*. The only safe conclusion to draw is that excesses of all kinds and on either side aroused his moral indignation, all the more since Tartuffe, though he gives evidence of being an adept in the casuistic reasoning of the Jesuits, knows how to use for his own advantage the pietistic vocabulary of the Jansenists. The aim of Molière evidently was an assault on hypocrisy in all its manifestations, and though he made use of the lines of attack opened up by Pascal, no one sector order was the direct object of his campaign. And curiously enough, showing the breadth of Molière's conception, both Jesuits and Jansenists in turn accused each other of having sat for the picture.

The play aroused also the antipathy of true piety. Orgon and Mme Pernelle are both sincere and become the dupes of their own religious zeal quite as much as of the machinations of Tartuffe. Here could be seen a covered attack against religion in its very essence, and this shocked the sensibilities of those honest souls not directly concerned in the religious controversies that stirred the hearts. In addition, Tartuffe, in his capacity as confident of Orgon resembled the spiritual adviser, and the repulsive picture which Molière had drawn was capable of leading the faithful astray, of making them doubt the sincerity of others accepted in similar confidence, and of thus undermining the very essence of the influence of the Church.

In view of these various inferences that were drawn from the moral of the play, it is important to understand the attitude of Molière in the construction of his plot. The various *Petitions* and the *Preface* should be read in this connection. His conception of comedy becomes evident from the first *Petition*. In the second he comments at length upon the reasons for the opposition which the play had encountered. Had he attacked religion and piety it would have passed without turmoil, as had been the case before. But here not what is sincere was held up to ridicule, but insincerity and hypocrisy, and the very fact that the opposition was so determined was proof of the accuracy of the picture.

In the *Preface* finally he explains at length his attitude in composing the play. He lays stress on the distinction which he has drawn between the hypocrite and the sanely devout Cléante and upon the fact that Tartuffe could not deceive the spectator for an instant, since his very appearance and all that he says or does give unmistakable evidence of his real nature. The whole question has ceased being a living one, and the play can now be seen or read without wounding religious susceptibilities. The manly religion of Cléante, the mouthpiece of Molière, stands in such clear contrast to the machinations of Tartuffe, that the unprejudiced judge cannot for a moment be deceived, and it is evident that true religion far from being injured by the play is in reality aggrandized and made more beautiful.

THE HISTORY OF THE PLAY

Among the many splendid entertainments offered by the young King Louis XIV to his court, that of the *Île enchantée*, which extended from the seventh to the thirteenth of May of the year 1664 at the château of Versailles, was one of the most extravagant. Just as Alcina in Ariosto's captivating poem the *Orlando Furioso* had attempted to make Roger and his companions on her enchanted island and in a marvelous palace forget the flight of time and the reality of life, so the king here wished, under similar conditions, to charm the men and women of his court. The story of this festivity, in which Molière and his troupe took a prominent part, does not belong within the limits of this Introduction. Besides taking part in the allegorical processions they repeated *Les Fâcheux* and *Le Mariage Forcé* and presented two new plays, *La Princesse d'Élide* and *Le Tartuffe*, of which the first three acts were played on May 12, the day before the end of the festivities.

Only surmises are possible with reference to the impression which the play produced, since the facts definitely known are meager. The king seems to have seen no cause for objection,[1] but other members of the court were shocked and brought their influence to bear upon him. Among this number was Anne of Austria, the queen mother. A devout Catholic, she saw danger to religion in the tone of the play and also feared that it might tend to weaken the influence which the Church was endeavoring to gain over the young king. Whether the Church took a decided stand in the matter at this early date it is difficult to decide, but as a matter of fact, before the seventeenth of May Molière had been informed of the king's order that no performance of *Tartuffe* should be given in public, and no efforts of Molière were able to alter the decision.

---

[1] Cp. the first *Petition*, in which Molière refers to the king's personal attitude.

The main motive of the opposition must, without question, be sought in the nature of the play, and Molière evidently understood the matter clearly, as can be seen from the *Preface* which appeared first with the edition of the play in 1669. Hypocrisy, using the garb and bearing of piety for the furtherance of selfish ends has been always present in the race, but the peculiar conditions in France during the seventeenth century, and the political influence of the Church had undoubtedly aided its development. Here, then, was the nucleus of an opposition which was quick to ally itself with honest devotion, whose sensibilities were touched by what might seem to be an attack against piety in general. Soon the opposition showed itself openly. Between July 28 and August 13 appeared a pamphlet by a curate of Paris by the name of Pierre Roullé entitled *Le Roy glorieux au monde ou Louis XIV le plus glorieux de ious les rois du monde* in which Molière was accused of having composed this play for the purpose of deriding Church and piety and declared worthy of being burned at the stake.[2]

In the meantime Molière utilized every opportunity to plead his cause. The king had gone from Versailles to Fontainebleau where our author and his troupe were invited to follow him again for the purpose of adding to the entertainment of the court. He said there from July 21 to August 13. The festivities seem to have been organized especially for the pleasure of Chigi, a nephew of the Pope, sent as legate on a special mission to the French capital. Molière saw the liberal spirit of this Italian dignitary, and appreciated the advantage to be gained from his support. He asked for permission to read the play to him, and was not deceived in his expectations. He now presented to the king his first *Petition*. Here he distinguishes between hypocrisy and true devotion, and calls attention to the sharp division which he has made between the two. He advances the statement that the prohibition to produce the play had been caused by the fact that certain Tartuffes at court had known how to prey upon the fine sensibilities of the king in religious matters to influence him to suppress a picture which they felt to be a true copy of themselves. Then he refers to the approbation which Chigi had bestowed upon the play, he denies the allegations of Roullé's pamphlet, and places the final decision into the hands of Louis XIV, whom, in the manner of the time, he compares to the all-wise God.

The hoped for favorable answer failed to come, but Molière evidently felt that a period of less rigor had set in. At the same time the curiosity to see the play which was capable to arouse such bitter animosity was constantly growing. Since it could not be put on the boards it was necessary to be content with private readings given by the author, and several such occasions are on record. In addition on September 25 the first three acts were played at Villers-Cotterets, at the

---

[2] Cp. the first *Petition*.

castle of the duke of Orléans, the brother of the king. The play found another advocate in the great Condé, and an anecdote relating to his protection is told by Molière at the end of the *Preface*. On November 29, Tartuffe, this time in four acts, was performed by his direction at the château de Raincy in connection with some festivities arranged by him for his son who not long before had married the daughter of the princess Palatine.

All these facts prove that after the first *Petition* the restrictions under which the play was suffering were considerably relaxed. Yet the old prohibition remained in force, and when Christine of Sweden wished to have *Tartuffe* performed for her in her castle in Rome in 1666, she was unable to enlist the aid of the French government.

In the meantime, the affairs of the troupe were far from satisfactory. *Don Juan*, Molière's next comedy, had suffered from the same opposition, and its performances had been interrupted. To indemnify him for the loss sustained, the king assigned him a pension of 6000 livres and authorized the company to take the name of *La Troupe du Roi*. The indecision of Louis XIV, made evident by this signal favor, is difficult to understand, but it seems to prove that Molière's first impression was correct and that he was not unfavorably disposed to the play. Various explanations have been given of this attitude. It has been maintained on the one hand that the king was chafing under the pressure which the austere Church party was bringing to bear upon him, and on the other that he enjoyed the attack on the Jansenists which the play seemed to contain.

In the following year (1667) the clouds appeared to lift for a moment. The king was embarking his campaign in Flanders, and before leaving Paris he seems to have given his consent for a public performance. At least Molière was under this impression[3] and arranged such a representation on August 5, 1667. From a desire to avoid further interruptions he had changed the text in various ways. Perhaps some of the alterations had been suggested by the king. The title had become *l'Imposteur*, and the name of Panulphe was substituted for that of Tartuffe. With his name he had also changed his character. He was now "un homme du monde" and wore the small hat, the long hair, the large collar, the lace and the sword of the man of society. Whether the spirit of the play had also been altered it is impossible to say, but it is certain that in various details the text was different from that which we know now.[4]

The relief was only temporary. On the following day M. de Lamoignon, president of the parliament, ordered the doors of the theater closed, and in spite of all that Molière could say or do he would

---

[3] Cp. the second *Petition*.
[4] Cp. the *Lettre sur la Comédie de l'Imposteur*.

not alter this decision. With this new prohibition the struggle began anew. Molière sent two of his actors, La Grange and La Thorillière to Lille where the king had his headquarters. He received them kindly, promised to look into the matter on his return, but did not interfere with Lamoignon's action. A few days later (August 11) the Church took a decided position in the discussion and Hardouin de Péréfixe, archbishop of Paris, promulgated a decree forbidding the reading or acting of the play within his diocese both in public and in private. Molière seems to have been completely disheartened by this overwhelming defeat. Sickness by which he was threatened may have complicated the condition. At any rate, the tone of the second *Petition* which he sent to the king at Lille is much more bitter than that of the first, and he even goes so far as to threaten his complete withdrawal from the theater, which certainly remained closed until September 25 of the same year. During this period there appeared the anonymous *Lettre sur la Comédie de l'Imposteur*,[5] an essay which defends the play and which is of prime importance for the study of the various phases through which it has passed. It has been maintained, though without proof, that Molière was personally directly concerned with its composition.

After this second defeat the history of the play offers no incidents of importance for our purposes during the space of nearly two years. The discouragement, which Molière felt at first, passed away. Even before Lamoignon's prohibitions he had written *Don Juan*. He now added *Le Médecin malgré lui* and *Le Misanthrope*, not to mention several other plays of minor importance. During the year 1668 he produced *Amphitryon* (January), *George Dandin* (July) and *L'Avare* (September).

In the meantime the long and tedious negotiations to which the Jansenist movement had given rise, had found a temporary solution in the *Paix de l'Église* (January 1, 1669), and it has been believed that the solution of these difficulties brought with it indirectly also the freedom of *Tartuffe*. Whether this point of view is correct remains an open question. Certainly the relation of the two events is quite superficial and the real reasons which determined Louis XIV to withdraw his objections to the play are quite obscure. The first public performance took place on February 5, 1669, and was a tremendous success. It was given twenty eight times in succession and remained one of the strongest attractions of Molière's troupe during the year. It appeared in print on March 15, 1669, together with a preface in which Molière indicated the history of the whole discussion and answered the objections to which the play had given rise.

---

[5] Cp. *Œuvres de Molière* in the *Grands Écrivains de la France*, vol. iv, p. 529 ff.

The animosity which *Tartuffe* had aroused was deeprooted. Louis
XIV could assure its existence on the stage, but he could not stop the
opposition to it. To be sure there were liberal minds like Saint-
Evremond who wrote to a friend '*Je viens de lire le Tartuffe, c'est le
chef d'œuvre de Molière. . . si je me sauve je lui devrai mon salut,*' but
there were others equally sincere who continued to protest. Bourdaloue,
who about this time began to preach in Paris, delivered two eloquent
sermons against the play, one on Hypocrisy, the other on True and
False Piety. This attack from the pulpit was continued by Bossuet, who
included the whole theater in his condemnation. Hostile criticism made
itself heard from time to time during the whole of the eighteenth and
even in the nineteenth century, but at the same time the true conception
of Molière became more and more clearly understood, and at present
critics do not hesitate to place the play not only in the first rank of
Molière's great character studies, but also among the very best
productions of the world's great literature.

THE SOURCES OF THE PLAY

Much patience and time has been spent in the search for the
probable sources and models of this masterpiece of the great comedian,
but the results so far have been of the most meager kind.

One or two points of contact with antecedent literature have been
indicated with Régnier's (1573-1613) Satire XIII in l. 1506, with
Boccaccio's eighth novel of book III in l. 966, but these are small and
do not affect the construction of the plot. There is, however, a passage
in Scarron's (1610-1660) novel *Les Hypocrites*, which is without
question the source of one of the characteristic scenes of Molière's
play, act III scene 6. Scarron here relates the story of an adventurer by
the name of Montufar and two women, one young the other old, who
under the semblance of religion plied a lucrative trade in Seville.
Montufar rented a house which he furnished with the greatest
simplicity, and dressed in austere and sombre garb all three worked
upon the religious susceptibilities of the inhabitants. He went to the
churches and prisons, made great show of almsgiving and religious
observances, all for the sake of his own gain and comfort, but with such
success that he and his companions soon gained the reputation of
saints. There happened to be a gentleman of Madrid in Seville at that
time, who formerly had been the lover of the younger of Montufar's
companions. Meeting them in front of one of the churches one day, he
became so incensed at their hypocrisy, that he broke through the
admiring and adoring crowd which surrounded them, and with a blow
of his fist sent Montufar reeling to the ground. The people, angered at
this action, rushed upon him and would have killed him; but Montufar
interceded and protected him. Then he approached the gentleman "*bien*

aise en son âme de le voir si maltraité, mais faisant paraître sur son visage qu'il en avait un extrême déplaisir, il le releva de terre où on l'avait jeté, l'embrassa et le baisa tout plein qu'il était de sang et de boue, et fit une rude réprimande au peuple. Je suis le méchant, disait-il à ceux qui le voulurent entendre; je suis le pécheur, je suis celui qui n'a jamais rien fait d'agréable aux yeux de Dieu. Pensez-vous, continuait-il, parce que vous me voyez vêtu en homme de bien, que je n'aie pas été toute ma vie un larron, le scandale des autres et la perdition de moi-même? Vous êtes trompés, mes frères, faites-moi le but de vos injures et de vos pierres, et tirez sur moi vos épées. - Après avoir dit ces paroles avec une fausse douceur, il s'alla jeter avec un zèle encore plus faux aux pieds de son ennemi, et, les lui baisant, non seulement il lui demanda pardon, mais aussi il alla ramasser son épée, son manteau et son chapeau, qui s'étaient perdus dans la confusion. Il les rajusta sur lui, et l'ayant ramené par la main jusqu'au bout de la rue, se sépara de lui après lui avoir donné plusieurs embrassements et autant de bénédictions. Le pauvre homme était comme enchanté, et de ce qu'il avait vu, et de ce qu'on lui avait fait, et si plein de confusion qu'on ne le vit pas paraître dans les rues tant que ses affaires le retinrent à Séville. Montufar, cependant, y avait gagné les cœurs de tout le monde par cet acte d'humilité contrefaite. Le peuple le regardait avec admiration, et les enfants criaient après lui: Au saint! au saint! comme ils eussent crié: Au renard! après son ennemi, s'ils l'eussent trouvé dans les rues. Dès ce temps-là, il commença de mener la vie du monde la plus heureuse. Le grand seigneur, le cavalier, le magistrat et le prélat l'avaient tous les jours à manger, à l'envi les uns des autres. Si on lui demandait son nom, il répondait qu'il était l'animal, la bête de charge, le cloaque d'ordures, le vaisseau d'iniquités, et autres pareils attributs que lui dictait sa dévotion étudiée. Il passait les jours sur les estrades avec les dames de la ville, se plaignant incessament à elles de sa tiédeur, qu'il n'était pas bien dans son néant, qu'il n'avait jamais assez de concentration de cœur ni de recueillement d'esprit, et enfin ne leur parlant jamais qu'en ce magnifique jargon de la cagoterie." In the meantime he continued his selfish aims and in secret lived magnificently on the alms which he devoted to the comfort of himself and his companions. Finally, however, he was denounced by his valet before justice, but suspecting the matter he managed to escape.

Comparison of this story with the play will show plainly the resemblance. But it has been so far the only evidence of indebtedness on Molière's part for the character of Tartuffe.

The attempt has been made to prove that Molière derived the idea of the play from some Italian compositions, notably the *Ipocrito* of Aretino and *Il Pedante*, a *commedia dell'arte* contained in Flaminio Scala's *Teatro delle Favole rappresentative* printed in 1611. The importance of the former was discussed by Moland in his book *Molière*

et la Comédie Italienne, pp. 209-224. The latter was brought forward as
a source by Vollhardt in Herrig's *Archiv für das Studium der neueren
Sprachen*, vol. 91, pp. 55 ff. In neither case has it been possible to
prove the point. The few similarities arise from the nature of the
subject.

The popular interpretation which saw in the play an argument in
the religious discussions of the time was not slow to find contemporary
authority for various portions of the plot. So the abbé Roquette, later
bishop of Autun, was supposed to have been partly copied in the
character of Tartuffe, a tradition which rests on an anecdote related by
the abbé de Choisy in his *Mémoirs*, and several references to him by
Mme de Sévigné.

It is particularly Orgon's famous *le pauvre homme* which has been
explained in various ways. Mme de Sévigné uses it in speaking of the
abbé Roquette, another anecdote attributes it to Louis XIV with
reference to Hardouin de Péréfixe, archbishop of Paris during the
campaign of the year 1662, and again Tallemant des Réaux relates a
story of a certain Père Joseph, in which the same words are used in
similar manner.

Another anecdote of Tallemant des Réaux[6] relates that a certain
abbé de Pons confessed his love to the famous Ninon de Lenclos in
words which give the spirit if not the words of 1. 966, and hence he
adds "*c'est l'original de Tartuffe.*" Elsewhere[7] he relates the following
story of M. Charpy, written before Tartuffe, probably in 1657. "*Il s'est
mis la dévotion dans la teste . . . . Or un jour qu'il estoit dans l'Eglise
des Quinze-Vingts, Mme Hausse, veuve de l'apoticaire de la Reyne, y
vint. . . . Il l'accosta et luy parla de dévotion avec tant d'emportement,
qu'il charma cette femme, qui est dévote. Elle le loge chez elle. Luy, qui
est si charitable qu'il aime son prochain comme luy-mesme, s'est mis à
aimer la petite Mme Patrocle, la fille de Mme Hansse: elle est femme
de chambre de la Reyne, et son mary est aussy à elle. Charpy se met si
bien dans l'esprit du mari et s'impatronise tellement de luy et de sa
femme, qu'il en a chassé tout le monde, et elle ne va en aucun lieu qu'il
n'y soit, ou bien le mary. Mme Hansse, qui a enfin ouvert les yeux, en a
averty son gendre; il a respondu que festoient des railleries, et prend
Çharpy pour le meilleur amy qu'il ayt au monde.*" The similarity with
the characters of Mme Pernelle and Orgon is striking, and since this
story was certainly written before the year 1664, it will be difficult not
to see here perhaps the most important of the contemporary sources of
Tartuffe.

From these notes the method of Molière becomes fairly clear. The
plot is probably of his own invention; his aim was to better man by

---

[6] *Les Historiettes*, vol. VI, p. 12.
[7] *Les Historiettes*, vol. VII, p. 213.

laying bare the foibles of his nature and as was always his custom *"il prend son bien où il le trouve."* Literature and gossip are mingled with direct observation to produce this masterly picture of human hypocrisy and credulity.

THE CHARACTERS AND THE PLAY

Critics are unanimous in declaring *Tartuffe* to be one of the most masterly productions of the world's dramatic literature. A few words are therefore in order setting forth the grounds upon which this claim is based. The play is the first of modern French character comedies. In a composition of this nature the plot is subordinated to the characters; in fact, it exists only for the purpose of setting forth their different aspects, and to a certain extent it grows out of them. Every scene of *Tartuffe* contains the hypocrit as the center, or is the result of his presence in the house of Orgon. He joins the subordinate to the principal action, and even the lover's quarrel (act II, sc. 4), which at first sight might appear independent, when looked at closely is seen to be the consequence of his scheming.

THE CHARACTERS. Tartuffe is clearly drawn. Steeped in hypocrisy and seeking his own gain, he shows himself in the clearest light in his relation to Elmire, but his cunning is none the less evident in the other scenes of the play. It is apparent in his entrance to Orgon's house and in the methods which he employs to maintain his influence there. It dominates his interview with Cléante, it dictates his casuistic reasoning with Elmire, and it stands out clearly in the end, when his heart is laid bare and he throws away the cloak under which he had hidden.

He is caught in the trap which Elmire sets for him, but the real cause of his defeat lies in his nature and is proof of the depth of Molière's analysis. His passion is stronger than his cunning, for it blinds him to the existence of danger. The climax thus springs not so much from the fact that Elmire outwits him, but that she understands his weak side and knows how to employ it for his undoing.

By the side of Tartuffe stand his servant Laurent and M. Loyal. There are hypocrits in all walks of life, and these cling together and work in harmony. Both are introduced for the purpose of placing the central character into a clearer light.

Near Tartuffe, and showing the side of human nature most open to the wiles of selfish cunning, stand Orgon and his mother. The former is a rich bourgeois, known at court. His home is the center of parties and receptions. During the troubles of the Fronde he had espoused the side of the king and gained respect and consideration. Yet he is a man of limited horizon, easily deceived by false appearances and a ready victim of Tartuffe, In fact he has become so completely dominated by him that he is ready to commit perjury, and openly declares that his wife and all his family count for nothing with him in comparison with the false ideals which he has imbibed from Tartuffe.

His character is emphasized by that of his mother, as simple-minded and blind as himself, and, indeed, the source of all his weakness.

Face to face with this group of hypocrits and their victims stand Elmire, Damis, Dorine and Cléante.

The figure of Elmire appears constructed mainly to embody the traits necessary for the undoing of Tartuffe. Her love for Orgon does not enter into the plot. She is, however, honest and upright, full of self-control, and, though conscious of her youth and charms, sincerely moral and above temptation. Her character is drawn with supreme skill and contains all the traits necessary for her share in the action.

Damis does not enter into the action sufficiently to demand a detailed delineation, though he stands out clearly. With all the impulsiveness of youth he is honest and open, and sees clearly the peril of the home.

Dorine, the soubrette of the cast, is one of the best figures of this type that Molière has drawn. She unites common sense and action. Like the ancient chorus, she gives on the one hand expression to the meaning of the action, and on the other she takes a prominent part in its development. She is thus as Sainte-Beuve has well expressed it the embodiment of Molière's muse, the personification of his humor, now bubbling over with laughter and again deep and serious as life.

Cléante is the mouthpiece of Molière, the *raisonneur* of the play. His speeches form the author's commentary of the action, and therefore deserve particular study. Yet he is not merely an empty figure. With his true and rational piety he becomes the natural counterpart of Tartuffe. His honesty cannot be questioned. He understands the hypocrit and tries to open Orgon's eyes. He is, however, not a man of action. Though he is fearless and speaks the truth regardless of consequences, he is satisfied with the exposure of wrong and does not consider it his duty to punish it. At the end, when the plot of *Tartuffe* is laid bare, it is he who counsels wisely and advises those who had suffered not to confuse true piety with the selfish use of it. Thus moderation is his main trait, and he represents the *honnête homme*, the healthy and wholesome element in society.

Mariane and Valère take part in the action only in subsidiary roles. The former is a dutiful daughter sacrificed by the blindness of her father, and the latter is the typical well-bred lover of the time.

THE EXPOSITION. The opening scene of the play is of unique art and has often been admired. Goethe called it the greatest and best of its kind. As Mme Pernelle answers one after the other of the members of the household, she characterizes them all. At the same time she permits

such a clear view of her own prejudices and limitations that the
spectator can without difficulty separate the true from the false, and
when the scene is over, the mental and moral background of the action
is clearly established. Almost immediately Orgon appears and confirms
the impression which has been created first in dialogue with Dorine (sc.
4), later with Cléante (sc. 5), and when the act closes, all the lines of the
plot have been laid and the simple action can take its course.

THE PLOT. The development of the plot is gradual but constant.
The spectator is now intent upon seeing the man around whom the
action centers, but before this can be, another act will show the ruin
which the selfishness of Tartuffe has already begun to work in Orgon's
family. All critics agree that the late entrance of Tartuffe on the scene
and the method of his appearance (1. 853) are evidences of the genius
of Molière. A character of this type cannot unfold itself gradually. He
must appear near the climax of the action and in a setting calculated to
confirm the impression that has been created. In fact all the worst
anticipations of the audience are realized at once. The climax of the
action is the attempt of Tartuffe on the honor of Elmire. The
impetuosity of Damis delays the dénouement for a moment and makes
room for a masterly scene in which Orgon and Tartuffe are for the first
time brought face to face before the audience so that the spectator can
see for himself the influence of the one upon the other. To prepare a
new scene in which the same climax would be reached again demanded
the skill of a genius, but Molière understood the difficulties and knew
how to solve them. Tartuffe and Elmire are brought together again, the
hypocrit is unmasked and the moment for the dénouement of the fifth
act has come.

L'ART DES PRÉPARATIONS. Molière is noted for the careful
attention which he bestows upon the logic of his plots even in the
minutest details. A few examples will serve to illustrate this phase of
his art. Tartuffe's passion for Elmire is mentioned three times by
Dorine, ll. 84, 837 ff., 876. before the two are brought together in act
III, sc. 3. Their second meeting in act IV, sc. 5 presented especial
difficulty. To make it possible, Elmire apparently shields Tartuffe
against Damis' accusation, and she presses him to favor the marriage of
Mariane and Valère, so that he might suppose that interest in him
prompts her action. Orgon's blindness in act III, sc. 6 appears natural
after his exhibition of mad infatuation for Tartuffe in act I, sc. 4. The
closet from which Damis can watch Tartuffe and Elmire, 1. 852, is
pointed out as a dangerous corner of the house by Orgon in 1. 430. The
king is ready to favor Orgon because of his support during the Fronde,
ll. 181 and 1939.

THE SOLUTION. The final act of the play cannot be included in this
general verdict of excellency. In fact adverse criticism was passed upon
it immediately after its appearance. The weakness begins with the

mention of the compromising box left in Orgon's safekeeping, ll. 1572 and 1576 ff. Though preparing the solution, it introduces a new motive at a time when the result should appear plainly the logical sum of the preceding action.

Critics have attempted to defend the solution itself, yet on the whole the opinion is adverse. The interest of the king in the action is unexpected. It should be noted, to be sure, that Tartuffe had gone to the king to denounce Orgon, l. 1921, and that the step had served to open the monarch's eyes, so that his verdict against the criminal is demanded by the claims of justice. But there is weakness in the arrangement, since Molière did not sufficiently emphasize the visit, and the logic of the action does not become apparent to the spectator. It can also not be affirmed with certainty that he intended the action to be thus understood. The fact remains that the last act does not belong to the original form of the play and that it was added at a time when Molère used every means within his power to obtain the protection of Louis XIV. Under these circumstances it is not at all impossible that he may have considered all the possibilities for solution which the plot offered, and rejected them all in favor of another that is not logical but which had the merit of gaining the support which the play needed to ensure its existence on the stage.

JOHN E. MATZKE

1906.

Moliere's Preface to "Tartuffe"

Here is a comedy about which much noise has been made; which was persecuted for years, while the persons it ridicules proved that they were much stronger in France than those I had hitherto laughed at. The marquises, the learned women, the luckless husbands, and the doctors had meekly borne their representation; in fact, they made believe to be amused, with the rest of the world, by the portraits made of them. But the hypocrites cannot bear ridicule. They were alarmed at once; and thought it monstrous that I should dare to make fun of their cant and attempt to decry a trade which so many honest folk are concerned in. That was a crime they could not pardon; and they all armed themselves against my comedy with dreadful fury. They took good care, however, not to attack it on the side where it wounded them; they are too politic for that; they know the ways of life too well to lay bare their real minds. Following their laudable custom, they hide their own interests behind the cause of God; "Tartuffe" they say, is an offence against religion. It is full of abominations from end to end; they see nothing in it but what deserves to be burned. Every syllable is impious; even the gestures are criminal; the merest glance, the slightest shaking of the head, the least step right or left, hide mysteries which they manage to explain to my injury.

In vain have I submitted my play to the judgment of friends, and to the criticism of all the world; the corrections I have made, the opinion of the king and queen, who have seen the comedy, the approbation of great princes and ministers of State who have publicly honored it with their presence, the testimony of good men who find it profitable,—all that is of no avail. My enemies will not desist; and to this day they prompt their zealous bigots, who cry out publicly, offer me pious insults, and charitably damn me.

I should care very little for what they say were it not for their cleverness in making me appear the enemy of that which I respect, and in winning to their side good men, whose genuine faith they work upon, and who, through the ardor which they truly feel for the cause of heaven, are open to the impressions my enemies seek to give them. It is this that obliges me to defend my cause. I desire to justify myself and my comedy in the minds of truly religious persons, whom I conjure, with all my heart, not to condemn these things before they see them, but, on the contrary, to lay aside all prejudice and not to serve the passions of those whose cant dishonors them.

If anyone will take pains to examine my comedy candidly, he will see that my intentions are wholly innocent; that the play does not, in any sense, laugh at those things which we ought to revere; that I have treated my subject with the precautions which its delicacy required; and that I have used all the art and all the care I possibly could in distinguishing the character of the hypocrite from that of truly pious men. For this very purpose, I employed two whole acts in preparing the way for my scoundrel. The audience is not kept for one moment in doubt; he is known for what he is from the start; and, from end to end, he does not say one word, he does not do one act, which will not show to the spectators the nature of a bad man, and bring into relief that of the good man to which I oppose him.

I know that these gentlemen insinuate, by way of answer, that the theatre is not the place to discuss these matters; but I ask, with all due deference to them, on what they base their theory. It is a proposition which they simply suppose; they have not tried to prove it in any way. It would not be difficult to prove to them, on the other hand, that comedy, among the ancients, had its origin in religion and made part of its Mysteries; that our neighbors the Spaniards never celebrate a church festival in which comedy does not take part; that even among ourselves, it owes its birth to the help of a religious fraternity who still own the Hôtel de Bourgogne, a place formerly set apart to represent the most important Mysteries of our faith; that we may still read comedies written in black-letter by a doctor of the Sorbonne; and finally, to go no farther, that in our own time the sacred plays of Monsieur de Corneille have been acted, to the admiration of all France.

If the purpose of comedy is to correct the vices of men, I do not see why some comedies should be privileged to do so, others not. To allow this would produce results far more dangerous to the State than any other. We have evidence that the stage has great virtue as a public corrective. But the finest shafts of serious morality are often less effective than those of satire; nothing corrects the majority of men so well as a picture of their faults. The strongest means of attacking vice is by exposing it to the laughter of the world. We can endure reproof, but we cannot endure ridicule. We are willing to be wicked, but not to be absurd.

I am reproached for putting pious language into the mouth of my impostor. Hey! how could I help it, if I truly represented the character of a hypocrite? It is enough, I think, to have made quite clear the criminal motives which make him say these things. I have cut out all sacred terms which might be painful when used by him in a shocking way. "But," says someone, "he proclaims, in the fourth act, a pernicious moral." Is not that moral a thing which is perpetually before our eyes? Does it reveal, in my comedy, a fact we do not know? Why should we fear that evils so generally detested should agreeably impress the mind, or that I make them dangerous by putting them on the stage and in the mouth of a known villain? There is no ground for such fear; and the comedy of "Tartuffe" must either be approved or other comedies must be condemned.

That, in fact, is the object of this attack, for never was there such inveighing against the stage. I cannot deny that there have been Fathers of the Church who condemned comedy; but no one can dispute that other reverend men have treated it more gently; therefore the weight of that censure is lessened by half; and all that can be deduced from this diversity of opinion among minds enlightened from the same source is that they have seen comedy from different points of view; some have considered it in its purity, while others looked only at its corruptions, and have confounded true comedy with villainous entertainments, justly called "spectacles of turpitude."

Now, inasmuch as we ought to discuss things, not words, and most of our contradictions come from not understanding each other and using the same words to cover opposite meanings, we have only to strip off the veil of ambiguity and look at what comedy really is, to see whether or not it is condemnable. We shall discover, I think, that being neither more nor less than a witty poem, reproving the faults of men by agreeable lessons, it cannot be censured without great injustice. If we are willing to listen to the testimony of antiquity it will tell us that the most celebrated philosophers praised comedy, even those who made profession of austere virtue and rebuked incessantly the vices of their age. It will show us that Aristotle devoted his evenings to the theatre, and took pains to reduce to precepts the art of writing comedy. It will also inform us that its greatest men, the first in dignity, made it their glory to write plays themselves; while others did not disdain to recite in public those they wrote; that Greece paid homage to the art by glorious prizes and the splendid theatres with which she honored it; and that in Rome the art was welcomed with extraordinary honors,—I do not mean in debauched and licentious Rome, under its emperors, but in the disciplined old Rome, under its consuls, in the days when Roman virtue was vigorous. I admit that there have been times when comedy became corrupt. What is there that the world does not corrupt? There is nothing so innocent that men will not foist sin into it; no art so wholesome but what they will reverse the intentions of it; nothing so good in itself that they will not put it to some bad use.

Medicine is a useful art; we all respect it as one of the most excellent things we have; and yet there have been times when it became odious; often it has been used to poison men. Philosophy is a gift from Heaven, bestowed upon us to lift our minds to the knowledge of God by the contemplation of his marvels in Nature; yet no one is ignorant how it has been turned from its true mission, and publicly used to sustain impiety. The holiest things are not protected from man's corruption; daily we see scoundrels misusing piety, and making it subserve the greatest crimes. But, for all that, we do not fail to make the proper distinctions; we do not involve, with false inference, the true excellence of the thing misused with the evil of its corrupters. We separate the harmful practice from the intention of the art itself; and, as we do not suppress medicine because Rome banished it, or philosophy because it was publicly condemned at Athens, neither ought we to forbid comedy because it was censured at one period of its history. That censure had its reasons, which exist no longer. Censure is now confined to what it sees; we ought not to draw it beyond the limit it has assigned to itself; it should not be suffered to go farther than it need and so involve the innocent with the guilty. The comedy that was formerly attacked is not the comedy we are now defending; and the public should be very careful not to confound the one with the other. They are two beings whose moral natures are entirely opposed. They have no connection with each other except in similarity of name. It would be a terrible injustice to condemn Olympia the virtuous woman because there was once another Olympia who was a wanton. Such judgments would create disorder in the world; nothing would be safe from condemnation; and, inasmuch as such rigor cannot be enforced, mercy should be shown to comedy, and approval given to plays in which integrity and instruction are seen to reign.

I know that there are minds whose delicacy cannot endure comedies of any kind; who say that the most virtuous are the most dangerous; that the passions therein depicted are all the more affecting because they are mingled with virtue, and that souls are moved to pity by such representations. I do not see that there is any crime in being moved by the sight of honest passion. The absolute insensibility to which these persons seek to raise our souls is a lofty stage of virtue; but I doubt if human nature has the strength to attain to such perfection, and I submit that it may be better to rectify and calm men's passions than seek to crush them altogether.

I will admit that there are places it were better to frequent than the theatre. If blame must indeed be cast on all things that do not look directly toward God, the stage must be one of them; and I should not complain were it condemned with all the rest. But let us suppose—what is true—that the exercises of religion must have intervals, and that men have need of relaxation and amusement; then I maintain that none more innocent can be found than that of comedy.

But I am writing too much. I will end with the remark of a great prince on the comedy of "Tartuffe."

Eight days after it was forbidden, a play was acted before the court entitled "Hermit Scaramouche" and the king, as he went out, said to the great prince whom I have mentioned: "I should like to know why the persons who are so scandalized at Moliere's comedy have never said a word against 'Scaramouche.'"

To which the prince replied: "The reason is that the comedy of 'Scaramouche' laughs at heaven and religion, about which those gentlemen care nothing at all; but Molière's comedy laughs at them; and that is a thing they cannot endure."

First Petition Presented to the King

ON THE COMEDY OF "TARTUFFE," WHICH HAD NOT YET BEEN REPRESENTED IN PUBLIC

SIRE,—The duty of comedy being to correct men while amusing them, I thought that, in the employ which I hold,[8] I could not do better than attack with ridiculous scenes the vices of my epoch; and as hypocrisy is one of the most common, troublesome, and dangerous of those vices, it came into my mind, Sire, that I should do no small service to all honest men in your kingdom if I wrote a comedy against hypocrites, and set forth, in a proper manner, the studied grimaces of those extravagantly pious folk, and the covert rascalities of those counterfeiters of devotion, who endeavor to impose on others by canting zeal and sophistical charity.

I wrote the comedy, Sire, with, as I think, all the care and

---

[8] That of leader of the "Troupe du Roi."

circumspection that the delicacy of the matter demanded; and the better to maintain the respect and esteem which we owe to all true piety, I made the character I had to deal with as plain as possible. I left nothing equivocal in my play. I took out all that might seem to confound good with evil, and used nothing in my picture but the special colors and essential features required to show at first sight an actual, unmistakable hypocrite.

Nevertheless all my precautions have been useless. Persons are relying, Sire, on the sensitiveness of your soul in matters of religion; and they have known how to take you on the only side on which you are takable,—I mean, that of your respect for sacred things. The Tartuffes have had the wit to find favor with your Majesty; in short, the originals have suppressed the copy, innocent as it is, and like as people thought it.

Though the suppression of my work has been a serious blow to me, my pain has been greatly softened by the manner in which your Majesty expressed yourself to me on the subject. I felt, Sire, that, your Majesty having had the kindness to declare you saw nothing to object to in the comedy which I am forbidden to produce, I had no cause whatever to complain.

But, notwithstanding this glorious declaration of the greatest king on earth and the most enlightened, in spite too of the approbation of Monseigneur the Legate and many of our own bishops, who, in the private readings which I have given before them of my work, agreed in the sentiments of your Majesty,—in spite, I say, of all that, a book has just appeared, written by the rector of the ——, which openly contradicts that august testimony. It is useless for your Majesty and Monseigneur the Legate and all the prelates to give your opinion; my comedy (though no one has seen it) is diabolical, and diabolical are my brains. I am a demon clothed in flesh and dressed like a man, a libertine free-thinker, an impious being, deserving of exemplary torture. It is not enough that fire should expiate my offences,—that would be letting me off too cheaply; the charitable zeal of the pious writer does not stop there; he insists that I shall receive no mercy from God; he is determined that I shall be damned—*that* is a settled matter.

The book, Sire, has been presented to your Majesty, who will no doubt perceive how grievous it must be for me to be daily exposed to the insults of these gentlemen, and what evil they can do me in the world by such calumnies, if they are tolerated; and also, what interest I have in freeing myself from such misstatements and proving to the public that my play is not in the least what they are trying to make it seem. I shall not say a word, Sire, of what I might ask in defense of my reputation, and to justify the innocence of my comedy in the eyes of the world; enlightened kings, like yourself, do not need to be shown what is desired; they see, like God, that which is needful for us, and know better than we what they ought to grant. It suffices me to put my cause in the hands of your Majesty, and I await, with respect, what it may please you to do in the matter.

Second Petition Presented to the King

IN HIS CAMP BEFORE THE TOWN OF LILLE IN FLANDERS; BY THE NAMED LA THORILLIÈRE AND LA GRANGE, COMEDIANS OF HIS MAJESTY AND COMPANIONS OF THE SIEUR MOLIÈRE; ON THE INJUNCTION ISSUED AUGUST 6, 1667, NOT TO PERFORM THE COMEDY OF "TARTUFFE" WITHOUT A FURTHER ORDER FROM HIS MAJESTY

SIRE,—It is a very bold thing in me to come and importune a great monarch in the midst of his glorious victories; but in the position in which I am placed, Sire, where shall I find protection except just here, where I seek it? Whom can I entreat to help me against the authority of a power which is crushing me, but the source of all power and authority, the just dispenser of absolute orders, the sovereign judge and master of all things?

My comedy, Sire, can be played here only through the kindness of Your Majesty. In vain have I produced it under the name of "The Impostor," and disguised that personage by the apparel of a man of the world; in vain have I given him a little hat, a bushy wig, a huge collar, with a sword, and lace all over his coat; in vain have I softened various parts and cut out carefully all that I thought capable of furnishing even a pretext to the celebrated originals, whose portraits I had endeavored to make; it was all to no purpose. The cabal is up in arms at the mere conjectures they have made about the thing. They have found means to mislead minds which, in other matters, profess that they are never misled. My comedy had no sooner appeared than it was blasted by an authority which we are forced to respect; and all that I was able to do in this crisis to save myself from the fury of the storm, was to say that your Majesty had been good enough to permit the performance, and that I therefore did not think myself obliged to ask permission of others, inasmuch as it was only your Majesty who had the power to withdraw that which I had.

I have no doubt, Sire, that the persons I depict in my comedy will use every effort against me with your Majesty, and will bring over to their side, as they have already done, many pious people, who are all the more easily misled because they judge others by themselves. My enemies have the art to give a fine coloring to their intentions; nevertheless, whatever they may pretend, it is not God's interests that move them. They have shown this plainly enough in the comedies they have allowed to be played many times in public without saying a word. Those comedies attacked only true religion and piety, for which these persons care very little; but mine attacks and laughs at *them*, and that is what they cannot bear. They will not forgive me for exposing their impostures to the eyes of the world; and, no doubt, they will tell your Majesty that everyone is scandalized by my comedy. But the real truth is, Sire, that all Paris is scandalized at the injunction put upon it. The most scrupulous persons thought the representation a useful one, and everyone is surprised that persons of eminent position should pay such deference to a class of men who ought to be the horror of the whole world, so opposite are they to the truth and piety they profess.

I respectfully await the judgment which your Majesty will deign to render on this subject; but it is very certain, Sire, that I shall have to give up writing comedies if the Tartuffes are to win the day. They will assume the right, from that moment, to persecute me more than ever, and to find fault with the most innocent things that come from my pen.

Deign of your goodness, Sire, to protect me against their envenomed hatred; and may I, on your return from this glorious campaign, refresh your Majesty after the fatigues of conquest, give you innocent pleasure after noble toil, and make the monarch laugh who makes all Europe tremble.

Third Petition Presented to the King

FEBRUARY 5, 1669

SIRE,—A very worthy doctor, whose patient I have the honor to be,[9] has promised, and is willing to go before a notary and swear, to make me live thirty years longer if I will obtain a favor from your Majesty. I told him as to his promise, that I did not want so much as that, and would be quite satisfied if he would bind himself not to kill me. The favor, Sire, is a canonry in your chapel-royal at Vincennes, made vacant by the death of ——.

Dare I ask this favor of your Majesty on the very day of the grand resurrection of "Tartuffe," resuscitated by your goodness? By that first favor I am reconciled to all godly people; by the second, if granted, I shall be reconciled with the doctors. For me, no doubt, these are too many great favors all at once; but perhaps they are not too many for your Majesty to grant; and I await, with some hope, the answer to my petition.

---

[9] His name was Mauvilain. The king said to Molière: "You have a doctor, what does he do for you?" "Sire," said Molière, "he comes to see me, we talk together, he prescribes remedies, I don't take them, and I get well." Molière obtained the canonry he asked for.

Tartuffe

[*Tartuffe, ou l'Imposteur.*]

A COMEDY IN FIVE ACTS

Translated by CURTIS HIDDEN PAGE

DRAMATIS PERSONAE

MADAME PERNELLE, *mother of Orgon.*
ORGON, *husband of Elmire.*
ELMIRE, *wife of Orgon.*
DAMIS, *son of Orgon.*
MARIANE, *daughter of Orgon, in love with Valere.*
CLEANTE, *brother-in-law of Orgon.*
TARTUFFE, *a hypocrite.*
DORINE, *Mariane's maid.*
M. LOYAL, *a bailiff.*
A Police Officer
FLIPOTTE, *Madame Pernelle's servant.*

The Scene is at Paris.

ACT I.

SCENE I.

[MADAME PERNELLE *and* FLIPOTTE, *her servant*; ELMIRE, MARIANE, CLEANTE, DAMIS, DORINE.]

MADAME PERNELLE. Come, come, Flipotte, and let me get away.
ELMIRE. You hurry so, I hardly can attend you.
MADAME PERNELLE. Then don't, my daughter-in law. Stay where
　　you are.
　　I can dispense with your polite attentions.
ELMIRE. We're only paying what is due you, mother.
　　Why must you go away in such a hurry?
MADAME PERNELLE. Because I can't endure your carryings-on,
　　And no one takes the slightest pains to please me.
　　I leave your house, I tell you, quite disgusted;
　　You do the opposite of my instructions;
　　You've no respect for anything; each one
　　Must have his say; it's perfect pandemonium.

DORINE. If . . .
MADAME PERNELLE. You're a servant wench, my girl, and much
Too full of gab, and too impertinent
And free with your advice on all occasions.
DAMIS. But . . .
MADAME PERNELLE. You're a fool, my boy—f, o, o, l
Just spells your name. Let grandma tell you that
I've said a hundred times to my poor son,
Your father, that you'd never come to good
Or give him anything but plague and torment.
MARIANE. I think . . .
MADAME PERNELLE. O dearie me, his little sister!
You're all demureness, butter wouldn't melt
In your mouth, one would think to look at you.
Still waters, though, they say . . . you know the proverb;
And I don't like your doings on the sly.
ELMIRE. But, mother . . .
MADAME PERNELLE. Daughter, by your leave, your conduct
In everything is altogether wrong;
You ought to set a good example for 'em;
Their dear departed mother did much better.
You are extravagant; and it offends me,
To see you always decked out like a princess.
A woman who would please her husband's eyes
Alone, wants no such wealth of fineries.
CLEANTE. But, madam, after all . . .
MADAME PERNELLE. Sir, as for you,
The lady's brother, I esteem you highly,
Love and respect you. But, sir, all the same,
If I were in my son's, her husband's, place,
I'd urgently entreat you not to come
Within our doors. You preach a way of living
That decent people cannot tolerate.
I'm rather frank with you; but that's my way—
I don't mince matters, when I mean a thing.
DAMIS. Mr. Tartuffe, your friend, is mighty lucky . . .
MADAME PERNELLE. He is a holy man, and must be heeded;
I can't endure, with any show of patience,
To hear a scatterbrains like you attack him.
DAMIS. What! Shall I let a bigot criticaster
Come and usurp a tyrant's power here?
And shall we never dare amuse ourselves
Till this fine gentleman deigns to consent?
DORINE. If we must hark to him, and heed his maxims,
There's not a thing we do but what's a crime;

He censures everything, this zealous carper.
MADAME PERNELLE. And all he censures is well censured, too.
He wants to guide you on the way to heaven;
My son should train you all to love him well.
DAMIS. No, madam, look you, nothing—not my father
Nor anything—can make me tolerate him.
I should belie my feelings not to say so.
His actions rouse my wrath at every turn;
And I foresee that there must come of it
An open rupture with this sneaking scoundrel.
DORINE. Besides, 'tis downright scandalous to see
This unknown upstart master of the house—
This vagabond, who hadn't, when he came,
Shoes to his feet, or clothing worth six farthings,
And who so far forgets his place, as now
To censure everything, and rule the roost!
MADAME PERNELLE. Eh! Mercy sakes alive! Things would go better
If all were governed by his pious orders.
DORINE. He passes for a saint in your opinion.
In fact, he's nothing but a hypocrite.
MADAME PERNELLE. Just listen to her tongue!
DORINE. I wouldn't trust him,
Nor yet his Lawrence, without bonds and surety.
MADAME PERNELLE. I don't know what the servant's character
May be; but I can guarantee the master
A holy man. You hate him and reject him
Because he tells home truths to all of you.
'Tis sin alone that moves his heart to anger,
And heaven's interest is his only motive.
DORINE. Of course. But why, especially of late,
Can he let nobody come near the house?
Is heaven offended at a civil call
That he should make so great a fuss about it?
I'll tell you, if you like, just what I think;

[*pointing to* ELMIRE.]

Upon my word, he's jealous of our mistress.
MADAME PERNELLE. You hold your tongue, and think what you are
        saying.
He's not alone in censuring these visits;
The turmoil that attends your sort of people,
Their carriages forever at the door,
And all their noisy footmen, flocked together,

Annoy the neighbourhood, and raise a scandal.
I'd gladly think there's nothing really wrong;
But it makes talk; and that's not as it should be.
CLEANTE. Eh! madam, can you hope to keep folk's tongues
From wagging? It would be a grievous thing
If, for the fear of idle talk about us,
We had to sacrifice our friends. No, no;
Even if we could bring ourselves to do it,
Think you that everyone would then be silenced?
Against backbiting there is no defence
So let us try to live in innocence,
To silly tattle pay no heed at all,
And leave the gossips free to vent their gall.
DORINE. Our neighbour Daphne, and her little husband,
Must be the ones who slander us, I'm thinking.
Those whose own conduct's most ridiculous,
Are always quickest to speak ill of others;
They never fail to seize at once upon
The slightest hint of any love affair,
And spread the news of it with glee, and give it
The character they'd have the world believe in.
By others' actions, painted in their colours,
They hope to justify their own; they think,
In the false hope of some resemblance, either
To make their own intrigues seem innocent,
Or else to make their neighbours share the blame
Which they are loaded with by everybody.
MADAME PERNELLE. These arguments are nothing to the purpose.
Orante, we all know, lives a perfect life;
Her thoughts are all of heaven; and I have heard
That she condemns the company you keep.
DORINE. O admirable pattern! Virtuous dame!
She lives the model of austerity;
But age has brought this piety upon her,
And she's a prude, now she can't help herself.
As long as she could capture men's attentions
She made the most of her advantages;
But, now she sees her beauty vanishing,
She wants to leave the world, that's leaving her,
And in the specious veil of haughty virtue
She'd hide the weakness of her worn-out charms.
That is the way with all your old coquettes;
They find it hard to see their lovers leave 'em;
And thus abandoned, their forlorn estate
Can find no occupation but a prude's.

These pious dames, in their austerity,
Must carp at everything, and pardon nothing.
They loudly blame their neighbours' way of living,
Not for religion's sake, but out of envy,
Because they can't endure to see another
Enjoy the pleasures age has weaned them from.
MADAME PERNELLE. [*to* ELMIRE.] There! That's the kind of
    rigmarole to please you,
Daughter-in-law. One never has a chance
To get a word in edgewise, at your house,
Because this lady holds the floor all day;
But none the less, I mean to have my say, too.
I tell you that my son did nothing wiser
In all his life, than take this godly man
Into his household; heaven sent him here,
In your great need, to make you all repent;
For your salvation, you must hearken to him;
He censures nothing but deserves his censure.
These visits, these assemblies, and these balls,
Are all inventions of the evil spirit.
You never hear a word of godliness
At them—but idle cackle, nonsense, flimflam.
Our neighbour often comes in for a share,
The talk flies fast, and scandal fills the air;
It makes a sober person's head go round,
At these assemblies, just to hear the sound
Of so much gab, with not a word to say;
And as a learned man remarked one day
Most aptly, 'tis the Tower of Babylon,
Where all, beyond all limit, babble on.
And just to tell you how this point came in . . .

    [*to* CLEANTE.]

So! Now the gentlemen must snicker, must he?
Go find fools like yourself to make you laugh
And don't . . .

    [*to* ELMIRE.]

Daughter, good-bye; not one word more.
As for this house, I leave the half unsaid;
But I shan't soon set foot in it again,

    [*cuffing* FLIPOTTE.]

Come, you! What makes you dream and stand agape,
Hussy! I'll warm your ears in proper shape!
March, trollop, march!

SCENE II.

[CLEANTE, DORINE.]

CLEANTE. I won't escort her down,
For fear she might fall foul of me again;
The good old lady . . .
DORINE. Bless us! What a pity
She shouldn't hear the way you speak of her!
She'd surely tell you you're too "good" by half,
And that she's not so "old" as all that, neither!
CLEANTE. How she got angry with us all for nothing!
And how she seems possessed with her Tartuffe!
DORINE. Her case is nothing, though, beside her son's!
To see him, you would say he's ten times worse!
His conduct in our late unpleasantness[10]
Had won him much esteem, and proved his courage
In service of his king; but now he's like
A man besotted, since he's been so taken
With this Tartuffe. He calls him brother, loves him
A hundred times as much as mother, son,
Daughter, and wife. He tells him all his secrets
And lets him guide his acts, and rule his conscience.
He fondles and embraces him; a sweetheart
Could not, I think, be loved more tenderly;
At table he must have the seat of honour,
While with delight our master sees him eat
As much as six men could; we must give up
The choicest tidbits to him; if he belches,

[*'tis a servant speaking.*][11]

Master exclaims: "God bless you!"—Oh, he dotes
Upon him! he's his universe, his hero;
He's lost in constant admiration, quotes him

---

[10] Referring to the rebellion called La Fronde, during the minority of Louis XIV.

[11] Moliere's note, inserted in the text of all the old editions. It is a curious illustration of the desire for uniformity and dignity of style in dramatic verse of the seventeenth century, that Moliere feels called on to apologize for a touch of realism like this. Indeed, these lines were even omitted when the play was given.

On all occasions, takes his trifling acts
For wonders, and his words for oracles.
The fellow knows his dupe, and makes the most on't,
He fools him with a hundred masks of virtue,
Gets money from him all the time by canting,
And takes upon himself to carp at us.
Even his silly coxcomb of a lackey
Makes it his business to instruct us too;
He comes with rolling eyes to preach at us,
And throws away our ribbons, rouge, and patches.
The wretch, the other day, tore up a kerchief
That he had found, pressed in the *Golden Legend*,
Calling it a horrid crime for us to mingle
The devil's finery with holy things.

SCENE III.

[ELMIRE, MARIANE, DAMIS, CLEANTE, DORINE.]

ELMIRE. [*to* CLEANTE.] You're very lucky to have missed the
    speech
    She gave us at the door. I see my husband
    Is home again. He hasn't seen me yet,
    So I'll go up and wait till he comes in.
CLEANTE. And I, to save time, will await him here;
    I'll merely say good-morning, and be gone.

SCENE IV.

[CLEANTE, DAMIS, DORINE.]

DAMIS. I wish you'd say a word to him about
    My sister's marriage; I suspect Tartuffe
    Opposes it, and puts my father up
    To all these wretched shifts. You know, besides,
    How nearly I'm concerned in it myself;
    If love unites my sister and Valere,
    I love his sister too; and if this marriage
    Were to . . .
DORINE. He's coming.

SCENE V.

[ORGON, CLEANTE, DORINE.]

ORGON. Ah! Good morning, brother.
CLEANTE. I was just going, but am glad to greet you.
Things are not far advanced yet, in the country?
ORGON. Dorine . . .

[*to* CLEANTE.]

Just wait a bit, please, brother-in-law.
Let me allay my first anxiety
By asking news about the family.

[*to* DORINE.]

Has everything gone well these last two days?
What's happening? And how is everybody?

DORINE. Madam had fever, and a splitting headache
Day before yesterday, all day and evening.
ORGON. And how about Tartuffe?
DORINE. Tartuffe? He's well;
He's mighty well; stout, fat, fair, rosy-lipped.
ORGON. Poor man!
DORINE. At evening she had nausea
And could't touch a single thing for supper,
Her headache still was so severe.
ORGON. And how
About Tartuffe?
DORINE. He supped alone, before her,
And unctuously ate up two partridges,
As well as half a leg o' mutton, deviled.
ORGON. Poor man!
DORINE. All night she couldn't get a wink
Of sleep, the fever racked her so; and we
Had to sit up with her till daylight.
ORGON. How
About Tartuffe?
DORINE. Gently inclined to slumber,
He left the table, went into his room,
Got himself straight into a good warm bed,
And slept quite undisturbed until next morning.

ORGON. Poor man!
DORINE. At last she let us all persuade her,
    And got up courage to be bled; and then
    She was relieved at once.
ORGON. And how about
    Tartuffe?
DORINE. He plucked up courage properly,
    Bravely entrenched his soul against all evils,
    And to replace the blood that she had lost,
    He drank at breakfast four huge draughts of wine.
ORGON. Poor man!
DORINE. So now they both are doing well;
    And I'll go straightway and inform my mistress
    How pleased you are at her recovery.

SCENE VI.

[ORGON, CLEANTE.]

CLEANTE. Brother, she ridicules you to your face;
    And I, though I don't want to make you angry,
    Must tell you candidly that she's quite right.
    Was such infatuation ever heard of?
    And can a man to-day have charms to make you
    Forget all else, relieve his poverty,
    Give him a home, and then . . . ?
ORGON. Stop there, good brother,
    You do not know the man you're speaking of.
CLEANTE. Since you will have it so, I do not know him;
    But after all, to tell what sort of man
    He is . . .
ORGON. Dear brother, you'd be charmed to know him;
    Your raptures over him would have no end.
    He is a man . . . who . . . ah! . . . in fact . . .a man
    Whoever does his will, knows perfect peace,
    And counts the whole world else, as so much dung.
    His converse has transformed me quite; he weans
    My heart from every friendship, teaches me
    To have no love for anything on earth;
    And I could see my brother, children, mother,
    And wife, all die, and never care—a snap.
CLEANTE. Your feelings are humane, I must say, brother!
ORGON. Ah! If you'd seen him, as I saw him first,
    You would have loved him just as much as I.
    He came to church each day, with contrite mien,

Kneeled, on both knees, right opposite my place,
And drew the eyes of all the congregation,
To watch the fervour of his prayers to heaven;
With deep-drawn sighs and great ejaculations,
He humbly kissed the earth at every moment;
And when I left the church, he ran before me
To give me holy water at the door.
I learned his poverty, and who he was,
By questioning his servant, who is like him,
And gave him gifts; but in his modesty
He always wanted to return a part.
"It is too much," he'd say, "too much by half;
I am not worthy of your pity." Then,
When I refused to take it back, he'd go,
Before my eyes, and give it to the poor.
At length heaven bade me take him to my home,
And since that day, all seems to prosper here.
He censures everything, and for my sake
He even takes great interest in my wife;
He lets me know who ogles her, and seems
Six times as jealous as I am myself.
You'd not believe how far his zeal can go:
He calls himself a sinner just for trifles;
The merest nothing is enough to shock him;
So much so, that the other day I heard him
Accuse himself for having, while at prayer,
In too much anger caught and killed a flea.
CLEANTE. Zounds, brother, you are mad, I think! Or else
You're making sport of me, with such a speech.
What are you driving at with all this nonsense . . . ?
ORGON. Brother, your language smacks of atheism;
And I suspect your soul's a little tainted
Therewith. I've preached to you a score of times
That you'll draw down some judgment on your head.
CLEANTE. That is the usual strain of all your kind;
They must have every one as blind as they.
They call you atheist if you have good eyes;
And if you don't adore their vain grimaces,
You've neither faith nor care for sacred things.
No, no; such talk can't frighten me; I know
What I am saying; heaven sees my heart.
We're not the dupes of all your canting mummers;
There are false heroes—and false devotees;
And as true heroes never are the ones
Who make much noise about their deeds of honour,

Just so true devotees, whom we should follow,
Are not the ones who make so much vain show.
What! Will you find no difference between
Hypocrisy and genuine devoutness?
And will you treat them both alike, and pay
The self-same honour both to masks and faces
Set artifice beside sincerity,
Confuse the semblance with reality,
Esteem a phantom like a living person,
And counterfeit as good as honest coin?
Men, for the most part, are strange creatures, truly!
You never find them keep the golden mean;
The limits of good sense, too narrow for them,
Must always be passed by, in each direction;
They often spoil the noblest things, because
They go too far, and push them to extremes.
I merely say this by the way, good brother.

ORGON. You are the sole expounder of the doctrine;
Wisdom shall die with you, no doubt, good brother,
You are the only wise, the sole enlightened,
The oracle, the Cato, of our age.
All men, compared to you, are downright fools.

CLEANTE. I'm not the sole expounder of the doctrine,
And wisdom shall not die with me, good brother.
But this I know, though it be all my knowledge,
That there's a difference 'twixt false and true.
And as I find no kind of hero more
To be admired than men of true religion,
Nothing more noble or more beautiful
Than is the holy zeal of true devoutness;
Just so I think there's naught more odious
Than whited sepulchres of outward unction,
Those barefaced charlatans, those hireling zealots,
Whose sacrilegious, treacherous pretence
Deceives at will, and with impunity
Makes mockery of all that men hold sacred;
Men who, enslaved to selfish interests,
Make trade and merchandise of godliness,
And try to purchase influence and office
With false eye-rollings and affected raptures;
Those men, I say, who with uncommon zeal
Seek their own fortunes on the road to heaven;
Who, skilled in prayer, have always much to ask,
And live at court to preach retirement;
Who reconcile religion with their vices,

Are quick to anger, vengeful, faithless, tricky,
And, to destroy a man, will have the boldness
To call their private grudge the cause of heaven;
All the more dangerous, since in their anger
They use against us weapons men revere,
And since they make the world applaud their passion,
And seek to stab us with a sacred sword.
There are too many of this canting kind.
Still, the sincere are easy to distinguish;
And many splendid patterns may be found,
In our own time, before our very eyes
Look at Ariston, Periandre, Oronte,
Alcidamas, Clitandre, and Polydore;
No one denies their claim to true religion;
Yet they're no braggadocios of virtue,
They do not make insufferable display,
And their religion's human, tractable;
They are not always judging all our actions,
They'd think such judgment savoured of presumption;
And, leaving pride of words to other men,
'Tis by their deeds alone they censure ours.
Evil appearances find little credit
With them; they even incline to think the best
Of others. No caballers, no intriguers,
They mind the business of their own right living.
They don't attack a sinner tooth and nail,
For sin's the only object of their hatred;
Nor are they over-zealous to attempt
Far more in heaven's behalf than heaven would have 'em.
That is my kind of man, that is true living,
That is the pattern we should set ourselves.
Your fellow was not fashioned on this model;
You're quite sincere in boasting of his zeal;
But you're deceived, I think, by false pretences.
ORGON. My dear good brother-in-law, have you quite done?
CLEANTE. Yes.
ORGON. I'm your humble servant.

[*starts to go.*]

CLEANTE. Just a word.
    We'll drop that other subject. But you know
    Valere has had the promise of your daughter.
ORGON. Yes.
CLEANTE. You had named the happy day.

ORGON. 'Tis true.
CLEANTE. Then why put off the celebration of it?
ORGON. I can't say.
CLEANTE. Can you have some other plan
    In mind?
ORGON. Perhaps.
CLEANTE. You mean to break your word?
ORGON. I don't say that.
CLEANTE. I hope no obstacle
    Can keep you from performing what you've promised.
ORGON. Well, that depends.
CLEANTE. Why must you beat about?
    Valere has sent me here to settle matters.
ORGON. Heaven be praised!
CLEANTE. What answer shall I take him?
ORGON. Why, anything you please.
CLEANTE. But we must know
    Your plans. What are they?
ORGON. I shall do the will
    Of Heaven.
CLEANTE. Come, be serious. You've given
    Your promise to Valere. Now will you keep it?
ORGON. Good-bye.
CLEANTE. [*alone.*] His love, methinks, has much to fear;
    I must go let him know what's happening here.

ACT II.

SCENE I.

[ORGON, MARIANE.]

ORGON. Now, Mariane.
MARIANE. Yes, father?
ORGON. Come; I'll tell you
    A secret.
MARIANE. Yes . . . What are you looking for?
ORGON. [*looking into a small closet-room.*]
    To see there's no one there to spy upon us;
    That little closet's mighty fit to hide in.
    There! We're all right now. Mariane, in you
    I've always found a daughter dutiful
    And gentle. So I've always love you dearly.
MARIANE. I'm grateful for your fatherly affection.
ORGON. Well spoken, daughter. Now, prove you deserve it

By doing as I wish in all respects.
MARIANE. To do so is the height of my ambition.
ORGON. Excellent well. What say you of—Tartuffe?
MARIANE. Who? I?
ORGON. Yes, you. Look to it how you answer.
MARIANE. Why! I'll say of him—anything you please.

SCENE II.

[ORGON, MARIANE, DORINE.]

[*coming in quietly and standing behind* ORGON, *so that he does not see her.*]

ORGON. Well spoken. A good girl. Say then, my daughter,
That all his person shines with noble merit,
That he has won your heart, and you would like
To have him, by my choice, become your husband.
Eh?
MARIANE. Eh?
ORGON. What say you?
MARIANE. Please, what did you say?
ORGON. What?
MARIANE. Surely I mistook you, sir?
ORGON. How now?
MARIANE. Who is it, father, you would have me say
Has won my heart, and I would like to have
Become my husband, by your choice?
ORGON. Tartuffe.
MARIANE. But, father, I protest it isn't true!
Why should you make me tell this dreadful lie?
ORGON. Because I mean to have it be the truth.
Let this suffice for you: I've settled it.
MARIANE. What, father, you would . . . ?
ORGON. Yes, child, I'm resolved
To graft Tartuffe into my family.
So he must be your husband. That I've settled.
And since your duty . .

[*seeing* DORINE.]

What are you doing there?
Your curiosity is keen, my girl,
To make you come eavesdropping on us so.

DORINE. Upon my word, I don't know how the rumour
    Got started—if 'twas guess-work or mere chance
    But I had heard already of this match,
    And treated it as utter stuff and nonsense.
ORGON. What! Is the thing incredible?
DORINE. So much so
    I don't believe it even from yourself, sir.
ORGON. I know a way to make you credit it.
DORINE. No, no, you're telling us a fairly tale!
ORGON. I'm telling you just what will happen shortly.
DORINE. Stuff!
ORGON. Daughter, what I say is in good earnest.
DORINE. There, there, don't take your father seriously;
    He's fooling.
ORGON. But I tell you . . .
DORINE. No. No use.
    They won't believe you.
ORGON. If I let my anger . . .
DORINE. Well, then, we do believe you; and the worse
    For you it is. What! Can a grown-up man
    With that expanse of beard across his face
    Be mad enough to want . . .?
ORGON. You hark me:
    You've taken on yourself here in this house
    A sort of free familiarity
    That I don't like, I tell you frankly, girl.
DORINE. There, there, let's not get angry, sir, I beg you.
    But are you making game of everybody?
    Your daughter's not cut out for bigot's meat;
    And he has more important things to think of.
    Besides, what can you gain by such a match?
    How can a man of wealth, like you, go choose
    A wretched vagabond for son-in-law?
ORGON. You hold your tongue. And know, the less he has,
    The better cause have we to honour him.
    His poverty is honest poverty;
    It should exalt him more than worldly grandeur,
    For he has let himself be robbed of all,
    Through careless disregard of temporal things
    And fixed attachment to the things eternal.
    My help may set him on his feet again,
    Win back his property—a fair estate
    He has at home, so I'm informed—and prove him
    For what he is, a true-born gentleman.
DORINE. Yes, so he says himself. Such vanity

But ill accords with pious living, sir.
The man who cares for holiness alone
Should not so loudly boast his name and birth;
The humble ways of genuine devoutness
Brook not so much display of earthly pride.
Why should he be so vain? . . . But I offend you:
Let's leave his rank, then,—take the man himself:
Can you without compunction give a man
Like him possession of a girl like her?
Think what a scandal's sure to come of it!
Virtue is at the mercy of the fates,
When a girl's married to a man she hates;
The best intent to live an honest woman
Depends upon the husband's being human,
And men whose brows are pointed at afar
May thank themselves their wives are what they are.
For to be true is more than woman can,
With husbands built upon a certain plan;
And he who weds his child against her will
Owes heaven account for it, if she do ill.
Think then what perils wait on your design.
ORGON. [*to Mariane.*] So! I must learn what's what from her, you see!
DORINE. You might do worse than follow my advice.
ORGON. Daughter, we can't waste time upon this nonsense;
I know what's good for you, and I'm your father.
True, I had promised you to young Valere;
But, first, they tell me he's inclined to gamble,
And then, I fear his faith is not quite sound.
I haven't noticed that he's regular
At church.
DORINE. You'd have him run there just when you do.
Like those who go on purpose to be seen?
ORGON. I don't ask your opinion on the matter.
In short, the other is in Heaven's best graces,
And that is riches quite beyond compare.
This match will bring you every joy you long for;
'Twill be all steeped in sweetness and delight.
You'll live together, in your faithful loves,
Like two sweet children, like two turtle-doves;
You'll never fail to quarrel, scold, or tease,
And you may do with him whate'er you please.
DORINE. With him? Do naught but give him horns, I'll warrant.
ORGON. Out on thee, wench!
DORINE. I tell you he's cut out for't;
However great your daughter's virtue, sir,

His destiny is sure to prove the stronger.
ORGON. Have done with interrupting. Hold your tongue.
Don't poke your nose in other people's business.
DORINE. [*she keeps interrupting him, just as he turns and starts to speak to his daughter.*] If I make bold, sir, 'tis for your own good.
ORGON. You're too officious; pray you, hold your tongue.
DORINE. 'Tis love of you . . .
ORGON. I want none of your love.
DORINE. Then I will love you in your own despite.
ORGON. You will, eh?
DORINE. Yes, your honour's dear to me;
I can't endure to see you made the butt
Of all men's ridicule.
ORGON. Won't you be still?
DORINE. 'Twould be a sin to let you make this match.
ORGON. Won't you be still, I say, you impudent viper!
DORINE. What! you are pious, and you lose your temper?
ORGON. I'm all wrought up, with your confounded nonsense;
Now, once for all, I tell you hold your tongue.
DORINE. Then mum's the word; I'll take it out in thinking.
ORGON. Think all you please; but not a syllable
To me about it, or . . . you understand!

[*turning to his daughter.*]

As a wise father, I've considered all
With due deliberation.

DORINE. I'll go mad
If I can't speak.

[*she stops the instant he turns his head.*]

ORGON. Though he's no lady's man,
Tartuffe is well enough . . .
DORINE. A pretty phiz!
ORGON. So that, although you may not care at all
For his best qualities . . .
DORINE. A handsome dowry!

[ORGON *turns and stands in front of her, with arms folded, eyeing her.*]

Were I in her place, any man should rue it
Who married me by force, that's mighty certain;

I'd let him know, and that within a week,
A woman's vengeance isn't far to seek.

ORGON. [*to* DORINE.] So—nothing that I say has any weight?
DORINE. Eh? What's wrong now? I didn't speak to you.
ORGON. What were you doing?
DORINE. Talking to myself.
ORGON. Oh! Very well. [*aside.*] Her monstrous impudence
Must be chastised with one good slap in the face.

[*he stands ready to strike her, and, each time he speaks to his
daughter, he glances toward her; but she stands still and says
not a word.*][12]

ORGON. Daughter, you must approve of my design. . . .
Think of this husband . . . I have chosen for you. . .

[*to* DORINE.]

Why don't you talk to yourself?

DORINE. Nothing to say.
ORGON. One little word more.
DORINE. Oh, no, thanks. Not now.
ORGON. Sure, I'd have caught you.
DORINE. Faith, I'm no such fool.
ORGON. So, daughter, now obedience is the word;
You must accept my choice with reverence.
DORINE. [*running away.*]
You'd never catch me marrying such a creature.
ORGON. [*swinging his hand at her and missing her.*]
Daughter, you've such a pestilent hussy there
I can't live with her longer, without sin.

---

[12] As given at the Comedie francaise, the action is as follows: While Orgon says,
"You must approve of my design," Dorine is making signs to Mariane to resist his orders;
Orgon turns around suddenly; but Dorine quickly changes her gesture and with the hand
which she had lifted calmly arranges her hair and her cap. Orgon goes on, "Think of the
husband . . ." and stops before the middle of his sentence to turn and catch the beginning
of Dorine's gesture; but he is too quick this time, and Dorine stands looking at his furious
countenance with a sweet and gentle expression. He turns and goes on, and the obstinate
Dorine again lifts her hand behind his shoulder to urge Mariane to resistance: this time he
catches her; but just as he swings his shoulder to give her the promised blow, she stops
him by changing the intent of her gesture, and carefully picking from the top of his sleeve
a bit of fluff which she holds carefully between her fingers, then blows into the air, and
watches intently as it floats away. Orgon is paralysed by her innocence of expression, and
compelled to hide his rage.—Regnier, *Le Tartuffe des Comediens.*

I can't discuss things in the state I'm in.
My mind's so flustered by her insolent talk,
To calm myself, I must go take a walk.

SCENE III.

[MARIANE, DORINE.]

DORINE. Say, have you lost the tongue from out your head?
    And must I speak your role from A to Zed?
    You let them broach a project that's absurd,
    And don't oppose it with a single word!
MARIANE. What can I do? My father is the master.
DORINE. Do? Everything, to ward off such disaster.
MARIANE. But what?
DORINE. Tell him one doesn't love by proxy;
    Tell him you'll marry for yourself, not him;
    Since you're the one for whom the thing is done,
    You are the one, not he, the man must please;
    If his Tartuffe has charmed him so, why let him
    Just marry him himself—no one will hinder.
MARIANE. A father's rights are such, it seems to me,
    That I could never dare to say a word.
DORINE. Came, talk it out. Valere has asked your hand:
    Now do you love him, pray, or do you not?
MARIANE. Dorine! How can you wrong my love so much,
    And ask me such a question? Have I not
    A hundred times laid bare my heart to you?
    Do you know how ardently I love him?
DORINE. How do I know if heart and words agree,
    And if in honest truth you really love him?
MARIANE. Dorine, you wrong me greatly if you doubt it;
    I've shown my inmost feelings, all too plainly.
DORINE. So then, you love him?
MARIANE. Yes, devotedly.
DORINE. And he returns your love, apparently?
MARIANE. I think so.
DORINE. And you both alike are eager
    To be well married to each other?
MARIANE. Surely.
DORINE. Then what's your plan about this other match?
MARIANE. To kill myself, if it is forced upon me.
DORINE. Good! That's a remedy I hadn't thought of.
    Just die, and everything will be all right.
    This medicine is marvellous, indeed!

It drives me mad to hear folk talk such nonsense.
MARIANE. Oh dear, Dorine you get in such a temper!
You have no sympathy for people's troubles.
DORINE. I have no sympathy when folk talk nonsense,
And flatten out as you do, at a pinch.
MARIANE. But what can you expect?—if one is timid?—
DORINE. But what is love worth, if it has no courage?
MARIANE. Am I not constant in my love for him?
Is't not his place to win me from my father?
DORINE. But if your father is a crazy fool,
And quite bewitched with his Tartuffe? And breaks
His bounden word? Is that your lover's fault?
MARIANE. But shall I publicly refuse and scorn
This match, and make it plain that I'm in love?
Shall I cast off for him, whate'er he be,
Womanly modesty and filial duty?
You ask me to display my love in public . . . ?
DORINE. No, no, I ask you nothing. You shall be
Mister Tartuffe's; why, now I think of it,
I should be wrong to turn you from this marriage.
What cause can I have to oppose your wishes?
So fine a match! An excellent good match!
Mister Tartuffe! Oh ho! No mean proposal!
Mister Tartuffe, sure, take it all in all,
Is not a man to sneeze at—oh, by no means!
'Tis no small luck to be his happy spouse.
The whole world joins to sing his praise already;
He's noble—in his parish; handsome too;
Red ears and high complexion—oh, my lud!
You'll be too happy, sure, with him for husband.
MARIANE. Oh dear! . . .
DORINE. What joy and pride will fill your heart
To be the bride of such a handsome fellow!
MARIANE. Oh, stop, I beg you; try to find some way
To help break off the match. I quite give in,
I'm ready to do anything you say.
DORINE. No, no, a daughter must obey her father,
Though he should want to make her wed a monkey.
Besides, your fate is fine. What could be better!
You'll take the stage-coach to his little village,
And find it full of uncles and of cousins,
Whose conversation will delight you. Then
You'll be presented in their best society.
You'll even go to call, by way of welcome,
On Mrs. Bailiff, Mrs. Tax-Collector,

Who'll patronise you with a folding-stool.
There, once a year, at carnival, you'll have
Perhaps—a ball; with orchestra—two bag-pipes;
And sometimes a trained ape, and Punch and Judy;
Though if your husband . . .
MARIANE. Oh, you'll kill me. Please
Contrive to help me out with your advice.
DORINE. I thank you kindly.
MARIANE. Oh! Dorine, I beg you . . .
DORINE. To serve you right, this marriage must go through.
MARIANE. Dear girl!
DORINE. No.
MARIANE. If I say I love Valere . . .
DORINE. No, no. Tartuffe's your man, and you shall taste him.
MARIANE. You know I've always trusted you; now help me . . .
DORINE. No, you shall be, my faith! Tartuffified.
MARIANE. Well, then, since you've no pity for my fate
Let me take counsel only of despair;
It will advise and help and give me courage;
There's one sure cure, I know, for all my troubles.

[*she starts to go.*]

DORINE. There, there! Come back. I can't be angry long.
I must take pity on you, after all.
MARIANE. Oh, don't you see, Dorine, if I must bear
This martyrdom, I certainly shall die.
DORINE. Now don't you fret. We'll surely find some way.
To hinder this . . . But here's Valere, your lover.

SCENE IV.

[VALERE, MARIANE, DORINE.]

VALERE. Madam, a piece of news—quite new to me—
Has just come out, and very fine it is.
MARIANE. What piece of news?
VALERE. Your marriage with Tartuffe.
MARIANE. 'Tis true my father has this plan in mind.
VALERE. Your father, madam . . .
MARIANE. Yes, he's changed his plans,
And did but now propose it to me.
VALERE. What!
Seriously?
MARIANE. Yes, he was serious,

And openly insisted on the match.
VALERE. And what's your resolution in the matter,
   Madam?
MARIANE. I don't know.
VALERE. That's a pretty answer.
   You don't know?
MARIANE. No.
VALERE. No?
MARIANE. What do you advise?
VALERE. I? My advice is, marry him, by all means.
MARIANE. That's your advice?
VALERE. Yes.
MARIANE. Do you mean it?
VALERE. Surely.
   A splendid choice, and worthy of your acceptance.
MARIANE. Oh, very well, sir! I shall take your counsel.
VALERE. You'll find no trouble taking it, I warrant.
MARIANE. No more than you did giving it, be sure.
VALERE. I gave it, truly, to oblige you, madam.
MARIANE. And I shall take it to oblige you, sir.
DORINE. [*withdrawing to the back of the stage.*]
   Let's see what this affair will come to.
VALERE. So,
   That is your love? And it was all deceit
   When you . . .
MARIANE. I beg you, say no more of that.
   You told me, squarely, sir, I should accept
   The husband that is offered me; and I
   Will tell you squarely that I mean to do so,
   Since you have given me this good advice.
VALERE. Don't shield yourself with talk of my advice.
   You had your mind made up, that's evident;
   And now you're snatching at a trifling pretext
   To justify the breaking of your word.
MARIANE. Exactly so.
VALERE. Of course it is; your heart
   Has never known true love for me.
MARIANE. Alas!
   You're free to think so, if you please.
VALERE. Yes, yes,
   I'm free to think so; and my outraged love
   May yet forestall you in your perfidy,
   And offer elsewhere both my heart and hand.
MARIANE. No doubt of it; the love your high deserts
   May win . . .

VALERE. Good Lord, have done with my deserts!
　　I know I have but few, and you have proved it.
　　But I may find more kindness in another;
　　I know of someone, who'll not be ashamed
　　To take your leavings, and make up my loss.
MARIANE. The loss is not so great; you'll easily
　　Console yourself completely for this change.
VALERE. I'll try my best, that you may well believe.
　　When we're forgotten by a woman's heart,
　　Our pride is challenged; we, too, must forget;
　　Or if we cannot, must at least pretend to.
　　No other way can man such baseness prove,
　　As be a lover scorned, and still in love.
MARIANE. In faith, a high and noble sentiment.
VALERE. Yes; and it's one that all men must approve.
　　What! Would you have me keep my love alive,
　　And see you fly into another's arms
　　Before my very eyes; and never offer
　　To someone else the heart that you had scorned?
MARIANE. Oh, no, indeed! For my part, I could wish
　　That it were done already.
VALERE. What! You wish it?
MARIANE. Yes.
VALERE. This is insult heaped on injury;
　　I'll go at once and do as you desire.

[he takes a step or two as if to go away.]

MARIANE. Oh, very well then.
VALERE. *[turning back.]* But remember this.
　　'Twas you that drove me to this desperate pass.
MARIANE. Of course.
VALERE. *[turning back again.]*
　　And in the plan that I have formed
　　I only follow your example.
MARIANE. Yes.
VALERE. *[at the door.]* Enough; you shall be punctually obeyed.
MARIANE. So much the better.
VALERE. *[coming back again.]* This is once for all.
MARIANE. So be it, then.
VALERE. *[he goes toward the door, but just as he reaches it, turns
　　around.]* Eh?
MARIANE. What?
VALERE. You didn't call me?
MARIANE. I? You are dreaming.

VALERE. Very well, I'm gone.
Madam, farewell.

[*he walks slowly away.*]

MARIANE. Farewell, sir.
DORINE. I must say
You've lost your senses and both gone clean daft!
I've let you fight it out to the end o' the chapter
To see how far the thing could go. Oho, there,
Mister Valere!

[*she goes and seizes him by the arm, to stop him. He makes a great show of resistance.*]

VALERE. What do you want, Dorine?
DORINE. Come here.
VALERE. No, no, I'm quite beside myself.
Don't hinder me from doing as she wishes.
DORINE. Stop!
VALERE. No. You see, I'm fixed, resolved, determined.
DORINE. So!
MARIANE. [*aside.*] Since my presence pains him, makes him go,
I'd better go myself, and leave him free.
DORINE. [*leaving* VALERE, *and running after* MARIANE.]
Now t'other! Where are you going?
MARIANE. Let me be.
DORINE. Come back.
MARIANE. No, no, it isn't any use.
VALERE. [*aside.*] 'Tis clear the sight of me is torture to her;
No doubt, t'were better I should free her from it.
DORINE. [*leaving* MARIANE *and running after* VALERE.]
Same thing again! Deuce take you both, I say.
Now stop your fooling; come here, you; and you.

[*she pulls first one, then the other, toward the middle of the stage.*]

VALERE. [*to* DORINE.] What's your idea?
MARIANE. [*to* DORINE.] What can you mean to do?
DORINE. Set you to rights, and pull you out o' the scrape.

[*to* VALERE.]

Are you quite mad, to quarrel with her now?

VALERE. Didn't you hear the things she said to me?
DORINE. [*to* MARIANE.] Are you quite mad, to get in such a
   passion?
MARIANE. Didn't you see the way he treated me?
DORINE. Fools, both of you.

   [*to* VALERE.]

   She thinks of nothing else
   But to keep faith with you, I vouch for it.

   [*to* MARIANE.]

   And he loves none but you, and longs for nothing
   But just to marry you, I stake my life on't.

MARIANE. [*to* VALERE.] Why did you give me such advice then,
   pray?
VALERE. [*to* MARIANE.] Why ask for my advice on such a matter?
DORINE. You both are daft, I tell you. Here, your hands.

   [*to* VALERE.]

   Come, yours.

VALERE. [*giving* DORINE *his hand.*] What for?
DORINE. [*to* MARIANE.] Now, yours.
MARIANE. [*giving* DORINE *her hand.*] But what's the use?
DORINE. Oh, quick now, come along. There, both of you—
   You love each other better than you think.

   [VALERE *and* MARIANE *hold each other's hands some time
   without looking at each other.*]

VALERE. [*at last turning toward* MARIANE.] Come, don't be so
      ungracious now about it;
   Look at a man as if you didn't hate him.

   [MARIANE *looks sideways toward* VALERE, *with just a bit of a
   smile.*]

DORINE. My faith and troth, what fools these lovers be!
VALERE. [*to* MARIANE.] But come now, have I not a just complaint?
   And truly, are you not a wicked creature
   To take delight in saying what would pain me?

MARIANE. And are you not yourself the most ungrateful . . . ?
DORINE. Leave this discussion till another time;
    Now, think how you'll stave off this plaguey marriage.
MARIANE. Then tell us how to go about it.
DORINE. Well,
    We'll try all sorts of ways.

[*to* MARIANE.]

Your father's daft;

[*to* VALERE.]

This plan is nonsense.

[*to* MARIANE.]

You had better humour
His notions by a semblance of consent,
So that in case of danger, you can still
Find means to block the marriage by delay.
If you gain time, the rest is easy, trust me.
One day you'll fool them with a sudden illness,
Causing delay; another day, ill omens:
You've met a funeral, or broke a mirror,
Or dreamed of muddy water. Best of all,
They cannot marry you to anyone
Without your saying yes. But now, methinks,
They mustn't find you chattering together.

[*to* VALERE.]

You, go at once and set your friends at work
To make him keep his word to you; while we
Will bring the brother's influence to bear,
And get the step-mother on our side, too.
Good-bye.
VALERE. [*to* MARIANE.] Whatever efforts we may make,
    My greatest hope, be sure, must rest on you.
MARIANE. [*to* VALERE.] I cannot answer for my father's whims;
    But no one save Valere shall ever have me.
VALERE. You thrill me through with joy! Whatever comes . . .
DORINE. Oho! These lovers! Never done with prattling!
    Now go.
VALERE. [*starting to go, and coming back again.*] One last word . . .

DORINE. What a gabble and pother!
    Be off! By this door, you. And you, by t'other.

[she pushes them off, by the shoulders, in opposite directions.]

ACT III.

SCENE I.

[DAMIS, DORINE.]

DAMIS. May lightning strike me dead this very instant,
    May I be everywhere proclaimed a scoundrel,
    If any reverence or power shall stop me,
    And if I don't do straightway something desperate!
DORINE. I beg you, moderate this towering passion;
    Your father did but merely mention it.
    Not all things that are talked of turn to facts;
    The road is long, sometimes, from plans to acts.
DAMIS. No, I must end this paltry fellow's plots,
    And he shall hear from me a truth or two.
DORINE. So ho! Go slow now. Just you leave the fellow—
    Your father too—in your step-mother's hands.
    She has some influence with this Tartuffe,
    He makes a point of heeding all she says,
    And I suspect that he is fond of her.
    Would God 'twere true!—'Twould be the height of humour
    Now, she has sent for him, in your behalf,
    To sound him on this marriage, to find out
    What his ideas are, and to show him plainly
    What troubles he may cause, if he persists
    In giving countenance to this design.
    His man says, he's at prayers, I mustn't see him,
    But likewise says, he'll presently be down.
    So off with you, and let me wait for him.
DAMIS. I may be present at this interview.
DORINE. No, no! They must be left alone.
DAMIS. I won't
    So much as speak to him.
DORINE. Go on! We know you
    And your high tantrums. Just the way to spoil things!
    Be off.
DAMIS. No, I must see—I'll keep my temper.
DORINE. Out on you, what a plague! He's coming. Hide!

[DAMIS *goes and hides in the closet at the back of the stage.*]

SCENE II.

[TARTUFFE, DORINE.]

TARTUFFE. [*speaking to his valet, off the stage, as soon as he sees* DORINE *is there.*]
Lawrence, put up my hair-cloth shirt and scourge,
And pray that Heaven may shed its light upon you.
If any come to see me, say I'm gone
To share my alms among the prisoners.
DORINE. [*aside.*] What affectation and what showing off!
TARTUFFE. What do you want with me?
DORINE. To tell you . . .
TARTUFFE. [*taking a handkerchief from his pocket.*] Ah!
Before you speak, pray take this handkerchief.
DORINE. What?
TARTUFFE. Cover up that bosom, which I can't
Endure to look on. Things like that offend
Our souls, and fill our minds with sinful thoughts.
DORINE. Are you so tender to temptation, then,
And has the flesh such power upon your senses?
I don't know how you get in such a heat;
For my part, I am not so prone to lust,
And I could see you stripped from head to foot,
And all your hide not tempt me in the least.
TARTUFFE. Show in your speech some little modesty,
Or I must instantly take leave of you.
DORINE. No, no, I'll leave you to yourself; I've only
One thing to say: Madam will soon be down,
And begs the favour of a word with you.
TARTUFFE. Ah! Willingly.
DORINE. [*aside.*] How gentle all at once!
My faith, I still believe I've hit upon it.
TARTUFFE. Will she come soon?
DORINE. I think I hear her now.
Yes, here she is herself; I'll leave you with her.

SCENE III.

[ELMIRE, TARTUFFE.]

TARTUFFE. May Heaven's overflowing kindness ever
    Give you good health of body and of soul,
    And bless your days according to the wishes
    And prayers of its most humble votary!
ELMIRE. I'm very grateful for your pious wishes.
    But let's sit down, so we may talk at ease.
TARTUFFE. [*after sitting down.*]
    And how are you recovered from your illness?
ELMIRE. [*sitting down also.*]
    Quite well; the fever soon let go its hold.
TARTUFFE. My prayers, I fear, have not sufficient merit
    To have drawn down this favour from on high;
    But each entreaty that I made to Heaven
    Had for its object your recovery.
ELMIRE. You're too solicitous on my behalf.
TARTUFFE. We could not cherish your dear health too much;
    I would have given mine, to help restore it.
ELMIRE. That's pushing Christian charity too far;
    I owe you many thanks for so much kindness.
TARTUFFE. I do far less for you than you deserve.
ELMIRE. There is a matter that I wished to speak of
    In private; I am glad there's no one here
    To listen.
TARTUFFE. Madam, I am overjoyed.
    'Tis sweet to find myself alone with you.
    This is an opportunity I've asked
    Of Heaven, many a time; till now, in vain.
ELMIRE. All that I wish, is just a word from you,
    Quite frank and open, hiding nothing from me.

[DAMIS, *without their seeing him, opens the closet door halfway.*]

TARTUFFE. I too could wish, as Heaven's especial favour,
    To lay my soul quite open to your eyes,
    And swear to you, the trouble that I made
    About those visits which your charms attract,
    Does not result from any hatred toward you,
    But rather from a passionate devotion,
    And purest motives . . .
ELMIRE. That is how I take it,

I think 'tis my salvation that concerns you.
TARTUFFE. [*pressing her finger tips.*] Madam, 'tis so; and such is my
    devotion . . .
ELMIRE. Ouch! but you squeeze too hard.
TARTUFFE. Excess of zeal.
    In no way could I ever mean to hurt you,
    And I'd as soon . . .

[*he puts his hand on her knee.*]

ELMIRE. What's your hand doing there?
TARTUFFE. Feeling your gown; the stuff is very soft.
ELMIRE. Let be, I beg you; I am very ticklish.

[*she moves her chair away, and* TARTUFFE *brings his nearer.*]

TARTUFFE. [*handling the lace yoke of* ELMIRE'*s dress.*]
    Dear me how wonderful in workmanship
    This lace is! They do marvels, nowadays;
    Things of all kinds were never better made.
ELMIRE. Yes, very true. But let us come to business.
    They say my husband means to break his word.
    And marry Mariane to you. Is't so?
TARTUFFE. He did hint some such thing; but truly, madam,
    That's not the happiness I'm yearning after;
    I see elsewhere the sweet compelling charms
    Of such a joy as fills my every wish.
ELMIRE. You mean you cannot love terrestrial things.
TARTUFFE. The heart within my bosom is not stone.
ELMIRE. I well believe your sighs all tend to Heaven,
    And nothing here below can stay your thoughts.
TARTUFFE. Love for the beauty of eternal things
    Cannot destroy our love for earthly beauty;
    Our mortal senses well may be entranced
    By perfect works that Heaven has fashioned here.
    Its charms reflected shine in such as you,
    And in yourself, its rarest miracles;
    It has displayed such marvels in your face,
    That eyes are dazed, and hearts are rapt away;
    I could not look on you, the perfect creature,
    Without admiring Nature's great Creator,
    And feeling all my heart inflamed with love
    For you, His fairest image of Himself.
    At first I trembled lest this secret love
    Might be the Evil Spirit's artful snare;

I even schooled my heart to flee your beauty,
Thinking it was a bar to my salvation.
But soon, enlightened, O all lovely one,
I saw how this my passion may be blameless,
How I may make it fit with modesty,
And thus completely yield my heart to it.
'Tis I must own, a great presumption in me
To dare make you the offer of my heart;
My love hopes all things from your perfect goodness,
And nothing from my own poor weak endeavour.
You are my hope, my stay, my peace of heart;
On you depends my torment or my bliss;
And by your doom of judgment, I shall be
Blest, if you will; or damned, by your decree.

ELMIRE. Your declaration's turned most gallantly;
But truly, it is just a bit surprising.
You should have better armed your heart, methinks,
And taken thought somewhat on such a matter.
A pious man like you, known everywhere . . .

TARTUFFE. Though pious, I am none the less a man;
And when a man beholds your heavenly charms,
The heart surrenders, and can think no more.
I know such words seem strange, coming from me;
But, madam, I'm no angel, after all;
If you condemn my frankly made avowal
You only have your charming self to blame.
Soon as I saw your more than human beauty,
You were thenceforth the sovereign of my soul;
Sweetness ineffable was in your eyes,
That took by storm my still resisting heart,
And conquered everything, fasts, prayers, and tears,
And turned my worship wholly to yourself.
My looks, my sighs, have spoke a thousand times;
Now, to express it all, my voice must speak.
If but you will look down with gracious favour
Upon the sorrows of your worthless slave,
If in your goodness you will give me comfort
And condescend unto my nothingness,
I'll ever pay you, O sweet miracle,
An unexampled worship and devotion.
Then too, with me your honour runs no risk;
With me you need not fear a public scandal.
These court gallants, that women are so fond of,
Are boastful of their acts, and vain in speech;
They always brag in public of their progress;

Soon as a favour's granted, they'll divulge it;
Their tattling tongues, if you but trust to them,
Will foul the altar where their hearts have worshipped.
But men like me are so discreet in love,
That you may trust their lasting secrecy.
The care we take to guard our own good name
May fully guarantee the one we love;
So you may find, with hearts like ours sincere,
Love without scandal, pleasure without fear.
ELMIRE. I've heard you through—your speech is clear, at least.
But don't you fear that I may take a fancy
To tell my husband of your gallant passion,
And that a prompt report of this affair
May somewhat change the friendship which he bears you?
TARTUFFE. I know that you're too good and generous,
That you will pardon my temerity,
Excuse, upon the score of human frailty,
The violence of passion that offends you,
And not forget, when you consult your mirror,
That I'm not blind, and man is made of flesh.
ELMIRE. Some women might do otherwise, perhaps,
But I am willing to employ discretion,
And not repeat the matter to my husband;
But in return, I'll ask one thing of you:
That you urge forward, frankly and sincerely,
The marriage of Valere to Mariane;
That you give up the unjust influence
By which you hope to win another's rights;
And . . .

SCENE IV.

[ELMIRE, DAMIS, TARTUFFE.]

DAMIS. [*coming out of the closet-room where he had been hiding.*]
No, I say! This thing must be made public.
I was just there, and overheard it all;
And Heaven's goodness must have brought me there
On purpose to confound this scoundrel's pride
And grant me means to take a signal vengeance
On his hypocrisy and arrogance,
And undeceive my father, showing up
The rascal caught at making love to you.
ELMIRE. No, no; it is enough if he reforms,
Endeavouring to deserve the favour shown him.

And since I've promised, do not you belie me.
'Tis not my way to make a public scandal;
An honest wife will scorn to heed such follies,
And never fret her husband's ears with them.
DAMIS. You've reasons of your own for acting thus;
And I have mine for doing otherwise.
To spare him now would be a mockery;
His bigot's pride has triumphed all too long
Over my righteous anger, and has caused
Far too much trouble in our family.
The rascal all too long has ruled my father,
And crossed my sister's love, and mine as well.
The traitor now must be unmasked before him:
And Providence has given me means to do it.
To Heaven I owe the opportunity,
And if I did not use it now I have it,
I should deserve to lose it once for all.
ELMIRE. Damis . . .
DAMIS. No, by your leave; I'll not be counselled.
I'm overjoyed. You needn't try to tell me
I must give up the pleasure of revenge.
I'll make an end of this affair at once;
And, to content me, here's my father now.

SCENE V.

[ORGON, ELMIRE, DAMIS, TARTUFFE.]

DAMIS. Father, we've news to welcome your arrival,
That's altogether novel, and surprising.
You are well paid for your caressing care,
And this fine gentleman rewards your love
Most handsomely, with zeal that seeks no less
Than your dishonour, as has now been proven.
I've just surprised him making to your wife
The shameful offer of a guilty love.
She, somewhat over gentle and discreet,
Insisted that the thing should be concealed;
But I will not condone such shamelessness,
Nor so far wrong you as to keep it secret.
ELMIRE. Yes, I believe a wife should never trouble
Her husband's peace of mind with such vain gossip;
A woman's honour does not hang on telling;
It is enough if she defend herself;
Or so I think; Damis, you'd not have spoken,

If you would but have heeded my advice.

SCENE VI.

[ORGON, DAMIS, TARTUFFE.]

ORGON. Just Heaven! Can what I hear be credited?
TARTUFFE. Yes, brother, I am wicked, I am guilty,
  A miserable sinner, steeped in evil,
  The greatest criminal that ever lived.
  Each moment of my life is stained with soilures;
  And all is but a mass of crime and filth;
  Heaven, for my punishment, I see it plainly,
  Would mortify me now. Whatever wrong
  They find to charge me with, I'll not deny it
  But guard against the pride of self-defence.
  Believe their stories, arm your wrath against me,
  And drive me like a villain from your house;
  I cannot have so great a share of shame
  But what I have deserved a greater still.
ORGON. [*to his son.*] You miscreant, can you dare, with such a
    falsehood,
  To try to stain the whiteness of his virtue?
DAMIS. What! The feigned meekness of this hypocrite
  Makes you discredit . . .
ORGON. Silence, cursed plague!
TARTUFFE. Ah! Let him speak; you chide him wrongfully;
  You'd do far better to believe his tales.
  Why favour me so much in such a matter?
  How can you know of what I'm capable?
  And should you trust my outward semblance, brother,
  Or judge therefrom that I'm the better man?
  No, no; you let appearances deceive you;
  I'm anything but what I'm thought to be,
  Alas! and though all men believe me godly,
  The simple truth is, I'm a worthless creature.

[*to* DAMIS.]

  Yes, my dear son, say on, and call me traitor,
  Abandoned scoundrel, thief, and murderer;
  Heap on me names yet more detestable,
  And I shall not gainsay you; I've deserved them;
  I'll bear this ignominy on my knees,
  To expiate in shame the crimes I've done.

ORGON. [*to* TARTUFFE.] Ah, brother, 'tis too much!

[*to his son.*]

> You'll not relent,
> You blackguard?

DAMIS. What! His talk can so deceive you . . .
ORGON. Silence, you scoundrel!

[*to* TARTUFFE.]

> Brother, rise, I beg you.

[*to his son.*]

> Infamous villain!

DAMIS. Can he . . .
ORGON. Silence!
DAMIS. What . . .
ORGON. Another word, I'll break your every bone.
TARTUFFE. Brother, in God's name, don't be angry with him!
> I'd rather bear myself the bitterest torture
> Than have him get a scratch on my account.
ORGON. [*to his son.*] Ungrateful monster!
TARTUFFE. Stop. Upon my knees
> I beg you pardon him . . .
ORGON. [*throwing himself on his knees too, and embracing*
>   TARTUFFE.]
> Alas! How can you?

[*to his son.*]

> Villain! Behold his goodness!

DAMIS. So . . .
ORGON. Be still.
DAMIS. What! I . . .
ORGON. Be still, I say. I know your motives
> For this attack. You hate him, all of you;
> Wife, children, servants, all let loose upon him,
> You have recourse to every shameful trick
> To drive this godly man out of my house;
> The more you strive to rid yourselves of him,
> The more I'll strive to make him stay with me;
> I'll have him straightway married to my daughter,
> Just to confound the pride of all of you.

DAMIS. What! Will you force her to accept his hand?
ORGON. Yes, and this very evening, to enrage you,
    Young rascal! Ah! I'll brave you all, and show you
    That I'm the master, and must be obeyed.
    Now, down upon your knees this instant, rogue,
    And take back what you said, and ask his pardon.
DAMIS. Who? I? Ask pardon of that cheating scoundrel . . . ?
ORGON. Do you resist, you beggar, and insult him?
    A cudgel, here! a cudgel!

[*to* TARTUFFE.]

Don't restrain me.

[*to his son.*]

Off with you! Leave my house this instant, sirrah,
    And never dare set foot in it again.
DAMIS. Yes, I will leave your house, but . . .
ORGON. Leave it quickly.
    You reprobate, I disinherit you,
    And give you, too, my curse into the bargain.

SCENE VII.

[ORGON, TARTUFFE.]

ORGON. What! So insult a saintly man of God!
TARTUFFE. Heaven, forgive him all the pain he gives me![13]

[*to* ORGON.]

Could you but know with what distress I see
Them try to vilify me to my brother!

---

[13] Some modern editions have adopted the reading, preserved by tradition as that of the earliest stage version:

Heaven, forgive him even as I forgive him!

Voltaire gives still another reading:

Heaven, forgive me even as I forgive him!

Whichever was the original version, it appears in none of the early editions, and Moliere probably felt forced to change it on account of its too close resemblance to the Biblical phrase.

ORGON. Ah!
TARTUFFE. The mere thought of such ingratitude
    Makes my soul suffer torture, bitterly . . .
    My horror at it . . . Ah! my heart's so full
    I cannot speak . . . I think I'll die of it.
ORGON. [*in tears, running to the door through which he drove away
    his son.*]
    Scoundrel! I wish I'd never let you go,
    But slain you on the spot with my own hand.

    [*to* TARTUFFE.]

    Brother, compose yourself, and don't be angry.
TARTUFFE. Nay, brother, let us end these painful quarrels.
    I see what troublous times I bring upon you,
    And think 'tis needful that I leave this house.
ORGON. What! You can't mean it?
TARTUFFE. Yes, they hate me here,
    And try, I find, to make you doubt my faith.
ORGON. What of it? Do you find I listen to them?
TARTUFFE. No doubt they won't stop there. These same reports
    You now reject, may some day win a hearing.
ORGON. No, brother, never.
TARTUFFE. Ah! my friend, a woman
    May easily mislead her husband's mind.
ORGON. No, no.
TARTUFFE. So let me quickly go away
    And thus remove all cause for such attacks.
ORGON. No, you shall stay; my life depends upon it.
TARTUFFE. Then I must mortify myself. And yet,
    If you should wish . . .
ORGON. No, never!
TARTUFFE. Very well, then;
    No more of that. But I shall rule my conduct
    To fit the case. Honour is delicate,
    And friendship binds me to forestall suspicion,
    Prevent all scandal, and avoid your wife.
ORGON. No, you shall haunt her, just to spite them all.
    'Tis my delight to set them in a rage;
    You shall be seen together at all hours
    And what is more, the better to defy them,
    I'll have no other heir but you; and straightway
    I'll go and make a deed of gift to you,
    Drawn in due form, of all my property.
    A good true friend, my son-in-law to be,

Is more to me than son, and wife, and kindred.
You will accept my offer, will you not?
TARTUFFE. Heaven's will be done in everything!
ORGON. Poor man!
 We'll go make haste to draw the deed aright,
 And then let envy burst itself with spite!

ACT IV.

SCENE I.

[CLEANTE, TARTUFFE.]

CLEANTE. Yes, it's become the talk of all the town,
 And make a stir that's scarcely to your credit;
 And I have met you, sir, most opportunely,
 To tell you in a word my frank opinion.
 Not to sift out this scandal to the bottom,
 Suppose the worst for us—suppose Damis
 Acted the traitor, and accused you falsely;
 Should not a Christian pardon this offence,
 And stifle in his heart all wish for vengeance?
 Should you permit that, for your petty quarrel,
 A son be driven from his father's house?
 I tell you yet again, and tell you frankly,
 Everyone, high or low, is scandalised;
 If you'll take my advice, you'll make it up,
 And not push matters to extremities.
 Make sacrifice to God of your resentment;
 Restore the son to favour with his father.
TARTUFFE. Alas! So far as I'm concerned, how gladly
 Would I do so! I bear him no ill will;
 I pardon all, lay nothing to his charge,
 And wish with all my heart that I might serve him;
 But Heaven's interests cannot allow it;
 If he returns, then I must leave the house.
 After his conduct, quite unparalleled,
 All intercourse between us would bring scandal;
 God knows what everyone's first thought would be!
 They would attribute it to merest scheming
 On my part—say that conscious of my guilt
 I feigned a Christian love for my accuser,
 But feared him in my heart, and hoped to win him
 And underhandedly secure his silence.
CLEANTE. You try to put us off with specious phrases;

But all your arguments are too far-fetched.
Why take upon yourself the cause of Heaven?
Does Heaven need our help to punish sinners?
Leave to itself the care of its own vengeance,
And keep in mind the pardon it commands us;
Besides, think somewhat less of men's opinions,
When you are following the will of Heaven.
Shall petty fear of what the world may think
Prevent the doing of a noble deed?
No!—let us always do as Heaven commands,
And not perplex our brains with further questions.
TARTUFFE. Already I have told you I forgive him;
And that is doing, sir, as Heaven commands.
But after this day's scandal and affront
Heaven does not order me to live with him.
CLEANTE. And does it order you to lend your ear
To what mere whim suggested to his father,
And to accept gift of his estates,
On which, in justice, you can make no claim?
TARTUFFE. No one who knows me, sir, can have the thought
That I am acting from a selfish motive.
The goods of this world have no charms for me;
I am not dazzled by their treacherous glamour;
And if I bring myself to take the gift
Which he insists on giving me, I do so,
To tell the truth, only because I fear
This whole estate may fall into bad hands,
And those to whom it comes may use it ill
And not employ it, as is my design,
For Heaven's glory and my neighbours' good.
CLEANTE. Eh, sir, give up these conscientious scruples
That well may cause a rightful heir's complaints.
Don't take so much upon yourself, but let him
Possess what's his, at his own risk and peril;
Consider, it were better he misused it,
Than you should be accused of robbing him.
I am astounded that unblushingly
You could allow such offers to be made!
Tell me—has true religion any maxim
That teaches us to rob the lawful heir?
If Heaven has made it quite impossible
Damis and you should live together here,
Were it not better you should quietly
And honourably withdraw, than let the son
Be driven out for your sake, dead against

All reason? 'Twould be giving, sir, believe me,
Such an example of your probity . . .
TARTUFFE. Sir, it is half-past three; certain devotions
Recall me to my closet; you'll forgive me
For leaving you so soon.
CLEANTE. [*alone.*] Ah!

SCENE II.

[ELMIRE, MARIANE, CLEANTE, DORINE.]

DORINE. [*to* CLEANTE.] Sir, we beg you
To help us all you can in her behalf;
She's suffering almost more than heart can bear;
This match her father means to make to-night
Drives her each moment to despair. He's coming.
Let us unite our efforts now, we beg you,
And try by strength or skill to change his purpose.

SCENE III.

[ORGON, ELMIRE, MARIANE, CLEANTE, DORINE.]

ORGON. So ho! I'm glad to find you all together.

[*to* MARIANE.]

Here is the contract that shall make you happy,
My dear. You know already what it means.
MARIANE. [*on her knees before* ORGON.] Father, I beg you, in the
name of Heaven
That knows my grief, and by whate'er can move you,
Relax a little your paternal rights,
And free my love from this obedience!
Oh, do not make me, by your harsh command,
Complain to Heaven you ever were my father;
Do not make wretched this poor life you gave me.
If, crossing that fond hope which I had formed,
You'll not permit me to belong to one
Whom I have dared to love, at least, I beg you
Upon my knees, oh, save me from the torment
Of being possessed by one whom I abhor!
And do not drive me to some desperate act
By exercising all your rights upon me.
ORGON. [*a little touched.*] Come, come, my heart, be firm! no human

weakness!

MARIANE. I am not jealous of your love for him;
Display it freely; give him your estate,
And if that's not enough, add all of mine;
I willingly agree, and give it up,
If only you'll not give him me, your daughter;
Oh, rather let a convent's rigid rule
Wear out the wretched days that Heaven allots me.

ORGON. These girls are ninnies!—always turning nuns
When fathers thwart their silly love-affairs.
Get on your feet! The more you hate to have him,
The more 'twill help you earn your soul's salvation.
So, mortify your senses by this marriage,
And don't vex me about it any more.

DORINE. But what . . . ?

ORGON. You hold your tongue, before your betters.
Don't dare to say a single word, I tell you.

CLEANTE. If you will let me answer, and advise . . .

ORGON. Brother, I value your advice most highly;
'Tis well thought out; no better can be had;
But you'll allow me—not to follow it.

ELMIRE. [*to her husband.*] I can't find words to cope with such a case;
Your blindness makes me quite astounded at you.
You are bewitched with him, to disbelieve
The things we tell you happened here to-day.

ORGON. I am your humble servant, and can see
Things, when they're plain as noses on folks' faces,
I know you're partial to my rascal son,
And didn't dare to disavow the trick
He tried to play on this poor man; besides,
You were too calm, to be believed; if that
Had happened, you'd have been far more disturbed.

ELMIRE. And must our honour always rush to arms
At the mere mention of illicit love?
Or can we answer no attack upon it
Except with blazing eyes and lips of scorn?
For my part, I just laugh away such nonsense;
I've no desire to make a loud to-do.
Our virtue should, I think, be gentle-natured;
Nor can I quite approve those savage prudes
Whose honour arms itself with teeth and claws
To tear men's eyes out at the slightest word.
Heaven preserve me from that kind of honour!
I like my virtue not to be a vixen,
And I believe a quiet cold rebuff

No less effective to repulse a lover.
ORGON. I know . . . and you can't throw me off the scent.
ELMIRE. Once more, I am astounded at your weakness;
I wonder what your unbelief would answer,
If I should let you see we've told the truth?
ORGON. See it?
ELMIRE. Yes.
ORGON. Nonsense.
ELMIRE. Come! If I should find
A way to make you see it clear as day?
ORGON. All rubbish.
ELMIRE. What a man! But answer me.
I'm not proposing now that you believe us;
But let's suppose that here, from proper hiding,
You should be made to see and hear all plainly;
What would you say then, to your man of virtue?
ORGON. Why, then, I'd say . . . say nothing. It can't be.
ELMIRE. Your error has endured too long already,
And quite too long you've branded me a liar.
I must at once, for my own satisfaction,
Make you a witness of the things we've told you.
ORGON. Amen! I take you at your word. We'll see
What tricks you have, and how you'll keep your promise.
ELMIRE. [*to* DORINE.] Send him to me.
DORINE. [*to* ELMIRE.] The man's a crafty codger,
Perhaps you'll find it difficult to catch him.
ELMIRE. [*to* DORINE.] Oh no! A lover's never hard to cheat,
And self-conceit leads straight to self-deceit.
Bid him come down to me.

[*to* CLEANTE *and* MARIANE.]

And you, withdraw.

Scene IV.

[ELMIRE, ORGON.]

ELMIRE. Bring up this table, and get under it.
ORGON. What?
ELMIRE. One essential is to hide you well.
ORGON. Why under there?
ELMIRE. Oh, dear! Do as I say;
I know what I'm about, as you shall see.
Get under, now, I tell you; and once there

Be careful no one either sees or hears you.
ORGON. I'm going a long way to humour you,
    I must say; but I'll see you through your scheme.
ELMIRE. And then you'll have, I think, no more to say.

[*to her husband, who is now under the table.*]

But mind, I'm going to meddle with strange matters;
Prepare yourself to be in no wise shocked.
Whatever I may say must pass, because
'Tis only to convince you, as I promised.
By wheedling speeches, since I'm forced to do it,
I'll make this hypocrite put off his mask,
Flatter the longings of his shameless passion,
And give free play to all his impudence.
But, since 'tis for your sake, to prove to you
His guilt, that I shall feign to share his love,
I can leave off as soon as you're convinced,
And things shall go no farther than you choose.
So, when you think they've gone quite far enough,
It is for you to stop his mad pursuit,
To spare your wife, and not expose me farther
Than you shall need, yourself, to undeceive you.
It is your own affair, and you must end it
When . . . Here he comes. Keep still, don't show yourself.

SCENE V.

[TARTUFFE, ELMIRE; ORGON (*under the table.*)]

TARTUFFE. They told me that you wished to see me here.
ELMIRE. Yes. I have secrets for your ear alone.
    But shut the door first, and look everywhere
    For fear of spies.

[TARTUFFE *goes and closes the door, and comes back.*]

We surely can't afford
Another scene like that we had just now;
Was ever anyone so caught before!
Damis did frighten me most terribly
On your account; you saw I did my best
To baffle his design, and calm his anger.
But I was so confused, I never thought
To contradict his story; still, thank Heaven,

Things turned out all the better, as it happened,
And now we're on an even safer footing.
The high esteem you're held in, laid the storm;
My husband can have no suspicion of you,
And even insists, to spite the scandal-mongers,
That we shall be together constantly;
So that is how, without the risk of blame,
I can be here locked up with you alone,
And can reveal to you my heart, perhaps
Only too ready to allow your passion.
TARTUFFE. Your words are somewhat hard to understand,
Madam; just now you used a different style.
ELMIRE. If that refusal has offended you,
How little do you know a woman's heart!
How ill you guess what it would have you know,
When it presents so feeble a defence!
Always, at first, our modesty resists
The tender feelings you inspire us with.
Whatever cause we find to justify
The love that masters us, we still must feel
Some little shame in owning it; and strive
To make as though we would not, when we would.
But from the very way we go about it
We let a lover know our heart surrenders,
The while our lips, for honour's sake, oppose
Our heart's desire, and in refusing promise.
I'm telling you my secret all too freely
And with too little heed to modesty.
But—now that I've made bold to speak—pray tell me.
Should I have tried to keep Damis from speaking,
Should I have heard the offer of your heart
So quietly, and suffered all your pleading,
And taken it just as I did—remember—
If such a declaration had not pleased me,
And, when I tried my utmost to persuade you
Not to accept the marriage that was talked of,
What should my earnestness have hinted to you
If not the interest that you've inspired,
And my chagrin, should such a match compel me
To share a heart I want all to myself?
TARTUFFE. 'Tis, past a doubt, the height of happiness,
To hear such words from lips we dote upon;
Their honeyed sweetness pours through all my senses
Long draughts of suavity ineffable.
My heart employs its utmost zeal to please you,

And counts your love its one beatitude;
And yet that heart must beg that you allow it
To doubt a little its felicity.
I well might think these words an honest trick
To make me break off this approaching marriage;
And if I may express myself quite plainly,
I cannot trust these too enchanting words
Until the granting of some little favour
I sigh for, shall assure me of their truth
And build within my soul, on firm foundations,
A lasting faith in your sweet charity.

ELMIRE. [*coughing to draw her husband's attention.*]
What! Must you go so fast?—and all at once
Exhaust the whole love of a woman's heart?
She does herself the violence to make
This dear confession of her love, and you
Are not yet satisfied, and will not be
Without the granting of her utmost favours?

TARTUFFE. The less a blessing is deserved, the less
We dare to hope for it; and words alone
Can ill assuage our love's desires. A fate
Too full of happiness, seems doubtful still;
We must enjoy it ere we can believe it.
And I, who know how little I deserve
Your goodness, doubt the fortunes of my daring;
So I shall trust to nothing, madam, till
You have convinced my love by something real.

ELMIRE. Ah! How your love enacts the tyrant's role,
And throws my mind into a strange confusion!
With what fierce sway it rules a conquered heart,
And violently will have its wishes granted!
What! Is there no escape from your pursuit?
No respite even?—not a breathing space?
Nay, is it decent to be so exacting,
And so abuse by urgency the weakness
You may discover in a woman's heart?

TARTUFFE. But if my worship wins your gracious favour,
Then why refuse me some sure proof thereof?

ELMIRE. But how can I consent to what you wish,
Without offending Heaven you talk so much of?

TARTUFFE. If Heaven is all that stands now in my way,
I'll easily remove that little hindrance;
Your heart need not hold back for such a trifle.

ELMIRE. But they affright us so with Heaven's commands!

TARTUFFE. I can dispel these foolish fears, dear madam;

I know the art of pacifying scruples
Heaven forbids, 'tis true, some satisfactions;
But we find means to make things right with Heaven.

[*'tis a scoundrel speaking.*][14]

There is a science, madam, that instructs us
How to enlarge the limits of our conscience
According to our various occasions,
And rectify the evil of the deed
According to our purity of motive.
I'll duly teach you all these secrets, madam;
You only need to let yourself be guided.
Content my wishes, have no fear at all;
I answer for't, and take the sin upon me.

[ELMIRE *coughs still louder.*]

Your cough is very bad.
ELMIRE. Yes, I'm in torture.
TARTUFFE. Would you accept this bit of licorice?
ELMIRE. The case is obstinate, I find; and all
    The licorice in the world will do no good.
TARTUFFE. 'Tis very trying.
ELMIRE. More than words can say.
TARTUFFE. In any case, your scruple's easily
    Removed. With me you're sure of secrecy,
    And there's no harm unless a thing is known.
    The public scandal is what brings offence,
    And secret sinning is not sin at all.
ELMIRE. [*after coughing again.*] So then, I see I must resolve to yield;
    I must consent to grant you everything,
    And cannot hope to give full satisfaction
    Or win full confidence, at lesser cost.
    No doubt 'tis very hard to come to this;
    'Tis quite against my will I go so far;
    But since I must be forced to it, since nothing
    That can be said suffices for belief,
    Since more convincing proof is still demanded,
    I must make up my mind to humour people.
    If my consent give reason for offence,
    So much the worse for him who forced me to it;
    The fault can surely not be counted mine.

---

[14] Moliere's note, in the original edition.

TARTUFFE. It need not, madam; and the thing itself . . .
ELMIRE. Open the door, I pray you, and just see
    Whether my husband's not there, in the hall.
TARTUFFE. Why take such care for him? Between ourselves,
    He is a man to lead round by the nose.
    He's capable of glorying in our meetings;
    I've fooled him so, he'd see all, and deny it.
ELMIRE. No matter; go, I beg you, look about,
    And carefully examine every corner.

SCENE VI.

[ORGON, ELMIRE.]

ORGON. [*crawling out from under the table.*] That is, I own, a man . . .
        abominable!
    I can't get over it; the whole thing floors me.
ELMIRE. What? You come out so soon? You cannot mean it!
    Get back under the table; 'tis not time yet;
    Wait till the end, to see, and make quite certain,
    And don't believe a thing on mere conjecture.
ORGON. Nothing more wicked e'er came out of Hell.
ELMIRE. Dear me! Don't go and credit things too lightly.
    No, let yourself be thoroughly convinced;
    Don't yield too soon, for fear you'll be mistaken.

[*as* TARTUFFE *enters, she makes her husband stand behind her.*]

SCENE VII.

[TARTUFFE, ELMIRE, ORGON.]

TARTUFFE. [*not seeing* ORGON.] All things conspire toward my
        satisfaction,
    Madam, I've searched the whole apartment through.
    There's no one here; and now my ravished soul . . .
ORGON. [*stopping him.*] Softly! You are too eager in your amours;
    You needn't be so passionate. Ah ha!
    My holy man! You want to put it on me!
    How is your soul abandoned to temptation!
    Marry my daughter, eh?—and want my wife, too?
    I doubted long enough if this was earnest,
    Expecting all the time the tone would change;
    But now the proof's been carried far enough;
    I'm satisfied, and ask no more, for my part.

ELMIRE. [*to* TARTUFFE.] 'Twas quite against my character to play
    This part; but I was forced to treat you so.
TARTUFFE. What? You believe . . . ?
ORGON. Come, now, no protestations.
    Get out from here, and make no fuss about it.
TARTUFFE. But my intent . . .
ORGON. That talk is out of season.
    You leave my house this instant.
TARTUFFE. You're the one
    To leave it, you who play the master here!
    This house belongs to me, I'll have you know,
    And show you plainly it's no use to turn
    To these low tricks, to pick a quarrel with me,
    And that you can't insult me at your pleasure,
    For I have wherewith to confound your lies,
    Avenge offended Heaven, and compel
    Those to repent who talk to me of leaving.

SCENE VIII.

[ELMIRE, ORGON.]

ELMIRE. What sort of speech is this? What can it mean?
ORGON. My faith, I'm dazed. This is no laughing matter.
ELMIRE. What?
ORGON. From his words I see my great mistake;
    The deed of gift is one thing troubles me.
ELMIRE. The deed of gift . . .
ORGON. Yes, that is past recall.
    But I've another thing to make me anxious.
ELMIRE. What's that?
ORGON. You shall know all. Let's see at once
    Whether a certain box is still upstairs.

ACT V.

SCENE I.

[ORGON, CLEANTE.]

CLEANTE. Whither away so fast?
ORGON. How should I know?
CLEANTE. Methinks we should begin by taking counsel
    To see what can be done to meet the case.
ORGON. I'm all worked up about that wretched box.

More than all else it drives me to despair.
CLEANTE. That box must hide some mighty mystery?
ORGON. Argas, my friend who is in trouble, brought it
    Himself, most secretly, and left it with me.
    He chose me, in his exile, for this trust;
    And on these documents, from what he said,
    I judge his life and property depend.
CLEANTE. How could you trust them to another's hands?
ORGON. By reason of a conscientious scruple.
    I went straight to my traitor, to confide
    In him; his sophistry made me believe
    That I must give the box to him to keep,
    So that, in case of search, I might deny
    My having it at all, and still, by favour
    Of this evasion, keep my conscience clear
    Even in taking oath against the truth.
CLEANTE. Your case is bad, so far as I can see;
    This deed of gift, this trusting of the secret
    To him, were both—to state my frank opinion—
    Steps that you took too lightly; he can lead you
    To any length, with these for hostages;
    And since he holds you at such disadvantage,
    You'd be still more imprudent, to provoke him;
    So you must go some gentler way about.
ORGON. What! Can a soul so base, a heart so false,
    Hide neath the semblance of such touching fervour?
    I took him in, a vagabond, a beggar! . . .
    'Tis too much! No more pious folk for me!
    I shall abhor them utterly forever,
    And henceforth treat them worse than any devil.
CLEANTE. So! There you go again, quite off the handle!
    In nothing do you keep an even temper.
    You never know what reason is, but always
    Jump first to one extreme, and then the other.
    You see your error, and you recognise
    That you've been cozened by a feigned zeal;
    But to make up for't, in the name of reason,
    Why should you plunge into a worse mistake,
    And find no difference in character
    Between a worthless scamp, and all good people?
    What! Just because a rascal boldly duped you
    With pompous show of false austerity,
    Must you needs have it everybody's like him,
    And no one's truly pious nowadays?
    Leave such conclusions to mere infidels;

Distinguish virtue from its counterfeit,
Don't give esteem too quickly, at a venture,
But try to keep, in this, the golden mean.
If you can help it, don't uphold imposture;
But do not rail at true devoutness, either;
And if you must fall into one extreme,
Then rather err again the other way.

SCENE II.

[DAMIS, ORGON, CLEANTE.]

DAMIS. What! father, can the scoundrel threaten you,
Forget the many benefits received,
And in his base abominable pride
Make of your very favours arms against you?
ORGON. Too true, my son. It tortures me to think on't.
DAMIS. Let me alone, I'll chop his ears off for him.
We must deal roundly with his insolence;
'Tis I must free you from him at a blow;
'Tis I, to set things right, must strike him down.
CLEANTE. Spoke like a true young man. Now just calm down,
And moderate your towering tantrums, will you?
We live in such an age, with such a king,
That violence can not advance our cause.

SCENE III.

[MADAME PERNELLE, ORGON, ELMIRE, CLEANTE,
MARIANE, DAMIS, DORINE.]

MADAME PERNELLE. What's this? I hear of fearful mysteries!
ORGON. Strange things indeed, for my own eyes to witness;
You see how I'm requited for my kindness,
I zealously receive a wretched beggar,
I lodge him, entertain him like my brother,
Load him with benefactions every day,
Give him my daughter, give him all my fortune:
And he meanwhile, the villain, rascal, wretch,
Tries with black treason to suborn my wife,
And not content with such a foul design,
He dares to menace me with my own favours,
And would make use of those advantages
Which my too foolish kindness armed him with,
To ruin me, to take my fortune from me,

And leave me in the state I saved him from.
DORINE. Poor man!
MADAME PERNELLE. My son, I cannot possibly
  Believe he could intend so black a deed.
ORGON. What?
MADAME PERNELLE. Worthy men are still the sport of envy.
ORGON. Mother, what do you mean by such a speech?
MADAME PERNELLE. There are strange goings-on about your
    house,
  And everybody knows your people hate him.
ORGON. What's that to do with what I tell you now?
MADAME PERNELLE. I always said, my son, when you were little:
  That virtue here below is hated ever;
  The envious may die, but envy never.
ORGON. What's that fine speech to do with present facts?
MADAME PERNELLE. Be sure, they've forged a hundred silly
  lies . . .
ORGON. I've told you once, I saw it all myself.
MADAME PERNELLE. For slanderers abound in calumnies . . .
ORGON. Mother, you'd make me damn my soul. I tell you
  I saw with my own eyes his shamelessness.
MADAME PERNELLE. Their tongues for spitting venom never lack,
  There's nothing here below they'll not attack.
ORGON. Your speech has not a single grain of sense.
  I saw it, harkee, saw it, with these eyes
  I saw—d'ye know what saw means?—must I say it
  A hundred times, and din it in your ears?
MADAME PERNELLE. My dear, appearances are oft deceiving,
  And seeing shouldn't always be believing.
ORGON. I'll go mad.
MADAME PERNELLE. False suspicions may delude,
  And good to evil oft is misconstrued.
ORGON. Must I construe as Christian charity
  The wish to kiss my wife!
MADAME PERNELLE. You must, at least,
  Have just foundation for accusing people,
  And wait until you see a thing for sure.
ORGON. The devil! How could I see any surer?
  Should I have waited till, before my eyes,
  He . . . No, you'll make me say things quite improper.
MADAME PERNELLE. In short, 'tis known too pure a zeal inflames
    him;
  And so, I cannot possibly conceive
  That he should try to do what's charged against him.
ORGON. If you were not my mother, I should say

Such things! . . . I know not what, I'm so enraged!
DORINE. [*to* ORGON.] Fortune has paid you fair, to be so doubted;
  You flouted our report, now yours is flouted.
CLEANTE. We're wasting time here in the merest trifling,
  Which we should rather use in taking measures
  To guard ourselves against the scoundrel's threats.
DAMIS. You think his impudence could go far?
ELMIRE. For one, I can't believe it possible;
  Why, his ingratitude would be too patent.
CLEANTE. Don't trust to that; he'll find abundant warrant
  To give good colour to his acts against you;
  And for less cause than this, a strong cabal
  Can make one's life a labyrinth of troubles.
  I tell you once again: armed as he is
  You never should have pushed him quite so far.
ORGON. True; yet what could I do? The rascal's pride
  Made me lose all control of my resentment.
CLEANTE. I wish with all my heart that some pretence
  Of peace could be patched up between you two
ELMIRE. If I had known what weapons he was armed with,
  I never should have raised such an alarm,
  And my . . .
ORGON. [*to* DORINE, *seeing* MR. LOYAL *come in.*] Who's coming
  now? Go quick, find out.
  I'm in a fine state to receive a visit!

SCENE IV.

[ORGON, MADAME PERNELLE, ELMIRE, MARIANE,
  CLEANTE, DAMIS, DORINE, MR. LOYAL.]

MR. LOYAL. [*to* DORINE, *at the back of the stage.*]
  Good day, good sister. Pray you, let me see
  The master of the house.
DORINE. He's occupied;
  I think he can see nobody at present.
MR. LOYAL. I'm not by way of being unwelcome here.
  My coming can, I think, nowise displease him;
  My errand will be found to his advantage.
DORINE. Your name, then?
MR. LOYAL. Tell him simply that his friend
  Mr. Tartuffe has sent me, for his goods . . .
DORINE. [*to* ORGON.] It is a man who comes, with civil manners,
  Sent by Tartuffe, he says, upon an errand
  That you'll be pleased with.

CLEANTE. [*to* ORGON.] Surely you must see him,
And find out who he is, and what he wants.
ORGON. [*to* CLEANTE.] Perhaps he's come to make it up between us:
How shall I treat him?
CLEANTE. You must not get angry;
And if he talks of reconciliation
Accept it.
MR. LOYAL. [*to* ORGON.] Sir, good-day. And Heaven send
Harm to your enemies, favour to you.
ORGON. [*aside to* CLEANTE.] This mild beginning suits with my
conjectures
And promises some compromise already.
MR. LOYAL. All of your house has long been dear to me;
I had the honour, sir, to serve your father.
ORGON. Sir, I am much ashamed, and ask your pardon
For not recalling now your face or name.
MR. LOYAL. My name is Loyal. I'm from Normandy.
My office is court-bailiff, in despite
Of envy; and for forty years, thank Heaven,
It's been my fortune to perform that office
With honour. So I've come, sir, by your leave
To render service of a certain writ . . .
ORGON. What, you are here to . . .
MR. LOYAL. Pray, sir, don't be angry.
'Tis nothing, sir, but just a little summons:—
Order to vacate, you and yours, this house,
Move out your furniture, make room for others,
And that without delay or putting off,
As needs must be . . .
ORGON. I? Leave this house?
MR. LOYAL. Yes, please, sir
The house is now, as you well know, of course,
Mr. Tartuffe's. And he, beyond dispute,
Of all your goods is henceforth lord and master
By virtue of a contract here attached,
Drawn in due form, and unassailable.
DAMIS. [*to* MR. LOYAL.] Your insolence is monstrous, and
astounding!
MR. LOYAL. [*to* DAMIS.] I have no business, sir, that touches you;

[*pointing to* ORGON.]

This is the gentleman. He's fair and courteous,
And knows too well a gentleman's behaviour
To wish in any wise to question justice.

ORGON. But . . .

MR. LOYAL. Sir, I know you would not for a million
    Wish to rebel; like a good citizen
    You'll let me put in force the court's decree.

DAMIS. Your long black gown may well, before you know it,
    Mister Court-bailiff, get a thorough beating.

MR. LOYAL. [*to* ORGON.] Sir, make your son be silent or withdraw.
    I should be loath to have to set things down,
    And see your names inscribed in my report.

DORINE. [*aside.*] This Mr. Loyal's looks are most disloyal.

MR. LOYAL. I have much feeling for respectable
    And honest folk like you, sir, and consented
    To serve these papers, only to oblige you,
    And thus prevent the choice of any other
    Who, less possessed of zeal for you than I am
    Might order matters in less gentle fashion.

ORGON. And how could one do worse than order people
    Out of their house?

MR. LOYAL. Why, we allow you time;
    And even will suspend until to-morrow
    The execution of the order, sir.
    I'll merely, without scandal, quietly,
    Come here and spend the night, with half a score
    Of officers; and just for form's sake, please,
    You'll bring your keys to me, before retiring.
    I will take care not to disturb your rest,
    And see there's no unseemly conduct here.
    But by to-morrow, and at early morning,
    You must make haste to move your least belongings;
    My men will help you—I have chosen strong ones
    To serve you, sir, in clearing out the house.
    No one could act more generously, I fancy,
    And, since I'm treating you with great indulgence,
    I beg you'll do as well by me, and see
    I'm not disturbed in my discharge of duty.

ORGON. I'd give this very minute, and not grudge it,
    The hundred best gold louis I have left,
    If I could just indulge myself, and land
    My fist, for one good square one, on his snout.

CLEANTE. [*aside to* ORGON.] Careful!—don't make things worse.

DAMIS. Such insolence!
    I hardly can restrain myself. My hands
    Are itching to be at him.

DORINE. By my faith,
    With such a fine broad back, good Mr. Loyal,

A little beating would become you well.

MR. LOYAL. My girl, such infamous words are actionable.

And warrants can be issued against women.

CLEANTE. [*to* MR. LOYAL.] Enough of this discussion, sir; have done.

Give us the paper, and then leave us, pray.

MR. LOYAL. Then *au revoir*. Heaven keep you from disaster!

ORGON. May Heaven confound you both, you and your master!

<h2 style="text-align:center">Scene V.</h2>

[ORGON, MADAME PERNELLE, ELMIRE, CLEANTE, MARIANE, DAMIS, DORINE.]

ORGON. Well, mother, am I right or am I not?

This writ may help you now to judge the matter.

Or don't you see his treason even yet?

MADAME PERNELLE. I'm all amazed, befuddled, and beflustered!

DORINE. [*to* ORGON.] You are quite wrong, you have no right to blame him;

This action only proves his good intentions.

Love for his neighbour makes his virtue perfect;

And knowing money is a root of evil,

In Christian charity, he'd take away

Whatever things may hinder your salvation.

ORGON. Be still. You always need to have that told you.

CLEANTE. [*to* ORGON.] Come, let us see what course you are to follow.

ELMIRE. Go and expose his bold ingratitude.

Such action must invalidate the contract;

His perfidy must now appear too black

To bring him the success that he expects.

<h2 style="text-align:center">Scene VI.</h2>

[VALERE, ORGON, MADAME PERNELLE, ELMIRE, CLEANTE, MARIANE, DAMIS, DORINE.]

VALERE. 'Tis with regret, sir, that I bring bad news;

But urgent danger forces me to do so.

A close and intimate friend of mine, who knows

The interest I take in what concerns you,

Has gone so far, for my sake, as to break

The secrecy that's due to state affairs,

And sent me word but now, that leaves you only

The one expedient of sudden flight.
The villain who so long imposed upon you,
Found means, an hour ago, to see the prince,
And to accuse you (among other things)
By putting in his hands the private strong-box
Of a state-criminal, whose guilty secret,
You, failing in your duty as a subject,
(He says) have kept. I know no more of it
Save that a warrant's drawn against you, sir,
And for the greater surety, that same rascal
Comes with the officer who must arrest you.
CLEANTE. His rights are armed; and this is how the scoundrel
Seeks to secure the property he claims.
ORGON. Man is a wicked animal, I'll own it!
VALERE. The least delay may still be fatal, sir.
I have my carriage, and a thousand louis,
Provided for your journey, at the door.
Let's lose no time; the bolt is swift to strike,
And such as only flight can save you from.
I'll be your guide to seek a place of safety,
And stay with you until you reach it, sir.
ORGON. How much I owe to your obliging care!
Another time must serve to thank you fitly;
And I pray Heaven to grant me so much favour
That I may some day recompense your service.
Good-bye; see to it, all of you . . .
CLEANTE. Come hurry;
We'll see to everything that's needful, brother.

SCENE VII.

[TARTUFFE, AN OFFICER, MADAME PERNELLE, ORGON,
ELMIRE, CLEANTE, MARIANE, VALERE, DAMIS,
DORINE.]

TARTUFFE. [*stopping* ORGON.] Softly, sir, softly; do not run so fast;
You haven't far to go to find your lodging;
By order of the prince, we here arrest you.
ORGON. Traitor! You saved this worst stroke for the last;
This crowns your perfidies, and ruins me.
TARTUFFE. I shall not be embittered by your insults,
For Heaven has taught me to endure all things.
CLEANTE. Your moderation, I must own, is great.
DAMIS. How shamelessly the wretch makes bold with Heaven!
TARTUFFE. Your ravings cannot move me; all my thought

Is but to do my duty.
MARIANE. You must claim
Great glory from this honourable act.
TARTUFFE. The act cannot be aught but honourable,
Coming from that high power which sends me here.
ORGON. Ungrateful wretch, do you forget 'twas I
That rescued you from utter misery?
TARTUFFE. I've not forgot some help you may have given;
But my first duty now is toward my prince.
The higher power of that most sacred claim
Must stifle in my heart all gratitude;
And to such puissant ties I'd sacrifice
My friend, my wife, my kindred, and myself.
ELMIRE. The hypocrite!
DORINE. How well he knows the trick
Of cloaking him with what we most revere!
CLEANTE. But if the motive that you make parade of
Is perfect as you say, why should it wait
To show itself, until the day he caught you
Soliciting his wife? How happens it
You have not thought to go inform against him
Until his honour forces him to drive you
Out of his house? And though I need not mention
That he'd just given you his whole estate,
Still, if you meant to treat him now as guilty,
How could you then consent to take his gift?
TARTUFFE. [*to the* OFFICER.] Pray, sir, deliver me from all this
    clamour;
Be good enough to carry out your order.
THE OFFICER. Yes, I've too long delayed its execution;
'Tis very fitting you should urge me to it;
So therefore, you must follow me at once
To prison, where you'll find your lodging ready.
TARTUFFE. Who? I, sir?
THE OFFICER. You.
TARTUFFE. By why to prison?
THE OFFICER. You
Are not the one to whom I owe account.
You, sir [*to* ORGON.], recover from your hot alarm.
Our prince is not a friend to double dealing,
His eyes can read men's inmost hearts, and all
The art of hypocrites cannot deceive him.
His sharp discernment sees things clear and true;
His mind cannot too easily be swayed,
For reason always holds the balance even.

He honours and exalts true piety,
But knows the false, and views it with disgust.
This fellow was by no means apt to fool him,
Far subtler snares have failed against his wisdom,
And his quick insight pierced immediately
The hidden baseness of this tortuous heart.
Accusing you, the knave betrayed himself,
And by true recompense of Heaven's justice
He stood revealed before our monarch's eyes
A scoundrel known before by other names,
Whose horrid crimes, detailed at length, might fill
A long-drawn history of many volumes.
Our monarch—to resolve you in a word—
Detesting his ingratitude and baseness,
Added this horror to his other crimes,
And sent me hither under his direction
To see his insolence out-top itself,
And force him then to give you satisfaction.
Your papers, which the traitor says are his,
I am to take from him, and give you back;
The deed of gift transferring your estate
Our monarch's sovereign will makes null and void;
And for the secret personal offence
Your friend involved you in, he pardons you:
Thus he rewards your recent zeal, displayed
In helping to maintain his rights, and shows
How well his heart, when it is least expected,
Knows how to recompense a noble deed,
And will not let true merit miss its due,
Remembering always rather good than evil.
DORINE. Now Heaven be praised!
MADAME PERNELLE. At last I breathe again.
ELMIRE. A happy outcome!
MARIANE. Who'd have dared to hope it?
ORGON. [*to* TARTUFFE, *who is being led by the officer.*] There
    traitor! Now you're . . .

SCENE VIII.

[MADAME PERNELLE, ORGON, ELMIRE, MARIANE,
    CLEANTE, VALERE, DAMIS, DORINE.]

CLEANTE. Brother, hold!—and don't
    Descend to such indignities, I beg you.
    Leave the poor wretch to his unhappy fate,

And let remorse oppress him, but not you.
Hope rather that his heart may now return
To virtue, hate his vice, reform his ways,
And win the pardon of our glorious prince;
While you must straightway go, and on your knees
Repay with thanks his noble generous kindness.
ORGON. Well said! We'll go, and at his feet kneel down,
With joy to thank him for his goodness shown;
And this first duty done, with honours due,
We'll then attend upon another, too.
With wedded happiness reward Valere,
And crown a lover noble and sincere.

[*curtain.*]

THE END